TWINKLE'S

big city knits

✳

TWINKLE'S

big city knits

Thirty-one chunky-chic designs

Wenlan Chia with Erica Roseman

POTTER
CRAFT

NEW YORK

Published in the United States by Potter Craft, an imprint of the Crown Publishing Group,
a division of Random House, Inc., New York.
www.crownpublishing.com
www.pottercraft.com

POTTER CRAFT and colophon and POTTER
and colophon are registered trademarks of Random House, Inc.

Library of Congress Cataloging-in-Publication Data
Chia, Wenlan.
  Twinkle's big city knits : 31 chunky-chic designs / Wenlan Chia — 1st ed.
     p. cm.
  ISBN-13: 978-0-307-34611-7
  ISBN-10: 0-307-34611-0
  1. Knitting. 2. Knitting—Patterns. I. Title.
  TT820.C48492 2006
  746.43'20432—dc22

                                        2006025315

Printed in China

10 9 8 7 6 5 4 3 2 1

First Edition

DESIGN: Gabriele Wilson

INSTRUCTION WRITER: Edie Eckman

TECH EDITOR: Karen Greenwald

PUBLIC RELATIONS: *Company Agenda*

HAIR: David Cruz for *Redken*

MAKE UP: Misuzu

CASTING: MAO

MODEL: Victoria Zuban at *Trump Management*

PROP STYLIST: Susan Balcunas

PHOTOGRAPHER: Arthur Adams

SPECIAL CAMEOS: Milan

Shot on location at Pier 59 Studios in New York City

For my mother

ACKNOWLEDGMENTS

I would like to thank everyone who has ever supported Twinkle, and for everything they have taught me, especially Rosy Ngo, Erica Roseman, Caroline Greeven, and Edie Eckman, for their talents and passion for perfection. Thanks as well to David Cruz, Misuzu, Roger Padilha, Victoria Zuban, Susan Balcunas, Naoko Aso, Liyia Wu, Jennifer Kao, Koon, Ashley, Wildy, Hana, and Arthur Adams, for collaborating on these beautiful pictures. Thanks also to Karen Greenward, Joe Kepferle, Lily Tran, Yu-lin Lee, Karina Peng, and Yuki Sekiya, for helping to put the book together. Thanks to Meilu Chen, who inspired me to pick up my first pair of knitting needles. Thanks to my parents, Hong-yeh Chia and Chu-yin Chia, and my sister, Ailan Chia, who are always encouraging and supporting me. Of course, the biggest thank-you goes to my husband, Bernard Lin, for everything we share in life.

DOWNTOWN

RESORT

NIGHT ON THE TOWN

SHOP THE TOWN

FOREWORD

For centuries, knitting has been an outlet for the creative expression for women—a hobby incorporating patience, a keen eye, and the desire to give to others.

And in the fashion world, where everything old is insistently new again, knitting has become chic. Over the past few years, knitting shops, knitting circles, and knitting classes have sprouted up all over the globe. While some might dismiss the knitting craze as the trendy hobby of the moment, it's not. The fad may wane, but knitting will always play a significant role in the inextricably connected worlds of craft and fashion.

There could not be a more timely moment for *Twinkle's Big City Knits*. Wenlan Chia has taken the craft and raised it to a high art—creating wonderfully whimsical, deliciously cozy pieces that are incredibly stylish and have an inexplicable air of sophistication mixed with utter simplicity. Within these pages, you will find impossibly cute pom-poms and sculptural cables in sweaters and accessories that will keep you looking babelicious whether you're uptown in the opera hall or downtown walking the dog. Knock 'em dead in the Karate Sweater or cozy up in the Rockefeller Sweater. Chia's pieces are the sort that make you want to curl up on the couch as much as they make you want to show them off to all your friends—turning your morning chore of dressing for the office into an exercise in self-expression.

Simply put, they twinkle.

In a way that can make any woman feel like a star.

— Dany Levy
Founder and editor-in-chief of dailycandy.com

INTRODUCTION

In *Twinkle's Big City Knits,* we've set out to capture the magical moment when fashion and knitting come to life at your fingertips. Here you'll discover the tremendous thrill and satisfaction of knitting something and wearing it that very day.

Knitters at every skill level will gain something valuable from this book. If you're a beginner who has only knit scarves, this book will inspire you to make a sweater you'll be proud to wear out on the town. For those of you who struggle to complete a project, it will encourage you to finish a sweater in one weekend. For all you avid knitters, it will send you off in unexpected design directions, rather than having you follow a pattern by rote. And if you're an old pro, it will expand your creative world in myriad new ways.

When women who wear Prada shoes and carry Balenciaga bags want to knit something for themselves, what do they make? We think this book holds the answer. It is for fashion lovers all over the world who want to create something as desirable as the designer clothes at Barneys New York. Only knitting costs less and is way more satisfying. And after seeing these amazing patterns, you'll be astounded at what you can accomplish with a simple cable stitch!

Twinkle knitwear is not only beautiful, it suits the busy lifestyle of the urban knitter. These projects knit up quickly, so there's no delayed gratification. Big stitches mean it takes you less time to complete a project. You'll finish a sweater in a weekend or in a week, with just a few hours' effort every night. Plus, the craft is soothing, relaxing, and oh-so therapeutic. Knitting is the ultimate escape. Most importantly, it satisfies your craving to create something uniquely your own.

As we styled the photos in *Twinkle's Big City Knits,* we thought about metropolitan women everywhere and how knitting these pieces could fit into their hectic schedules. Each chapter reflects one aspect of city life: From Balthazar brunches to shopping excursions, from St. Bart's vacations to glittering evenings at your favorite nightspots, we show you how making your own knitwear can dovetail with your busy lifestyle. My dog Milan—one of my own sources of inspiration— appears on each chapter opener and frames the topic at hand (or at paw, if you will). The thirty-one original Twinkle designs in this book range from beginner to advanced. It all comes together with technical tips, styling suggestions, and beauty bites—everything you need to know to go from pedestrian to show-stopping. But keep in mind that choosing the right color yarn is key. You know which colors play up your best features, so make sure to pick the ones that will bring out those gorgeous eyes, that glowing complexion, or the glam hairdo that halts traffic wherever you go.

My passion is chunky knits. I learned how to knit by making chunky sweaters and have crafted my professional reputation around them. They changed my life, and I hope they will enhance yours! Of course, knitting with bulky yarns has inherent challenges, but at the same time, it continues to surprise, fascinate, and astonish me. In working with these yarns, I have learned that the techniques for designing knitwear and woven fabrics are interchangeable. In these pages, I hope that you too will discover that knitting with chunkies opens up an array of amazing design possibilities.

Every knitter approaches her first seemingly difficult project with trepidation. Yet, oftentimes, this project sets the stage for a whole new—and utterly unforeseen—adventure in her journey as a knitter. As you finish a project that initially seemed beyond your grasp, you'll realize that your skills have improved and that you're ready to learn even more. In my own initial forays into knitting, serendipity also figured in. My first knitwear collection, which were the sweaters that launched Twinkle by Wenlan, was actually inspired by a school project.

Today, I continue to venture out in new directions, treating chunky knits as a novel fabric, a canvas on which I can paint my heart's desires. For me, the the key to knitting is not skill level or technical knowledge but the love for the clothes. Passion for fashion and design makes it happen!

Before starting each project, be sure you understand how to make all the stitches in the pattern. Naturally, this is difficult for the fashion addict who sees a sweater and must have it right away, but by practicing stitches and knitting with chunky yarn, you will learn techniques that can be used again and again. Eventually, your imagination will guide you as you start to make your own fabulous knit fashions. And through these exercises in creative needlework, you will come away with the empowering feeling that you can accomplish anything.

This is the spirit of knitting that I love!

—Wenlan

downtown: gorgeous, groovy girls

City sidewalks require smart style. The Twinkle knits in this chapter were designed to make their way through cool, chic crowds. Wearing them will cause traffic to stop and people to talk.

MIX AND MATCH Dare to pair delicate fabrics with Twinkle chunky knits. Sweaters add street savvy when worn over feminine fabrics like silk, charmeuse, or chiffon. WEAR IT YOUR WAY Customize your knits: extra-long, super-short, teeny-tiny, big buttons, pretty pom-poms—anything goes. LAYERS ARE LOVELY Chunky knit jackets and vests dazzle over printed dresses and skirts. It's the ultimate in boho chic! HIP AND HAPPENING HUES Winter white, dusty pink, teal green, and icy blue—all these subtle shades brighten cityscapes. Darker colors like blacks and grays add dimension to pretty, colorful dresses. DENIM TO DIE FOR Bring it down a notch, by pairing denims with sweaters and vests to create instant classic cool! FACE IT Loose, romantic tresses contrast with matte makeup and bedroom eyes to give you a self-assured yet feminine look. CHARM THEM Charms and pendants in quirky shapes and clever combinations add splash and pizzazz to downtown designs.

Circular knitting at its best!

Thinking knitters approach Twinkle's Groovy Sweater (Dress) as a three-dimensional sculpture knit with circular needles, not as two flat patterns joined together. The short-row technique makes the seamless neckline seem effortless. Crisscross cables, ribbing, and budding flowers pop on a purl stitch background.

THIS PATTERN STARTS ON PAGE 84.

groovy sweater{dress}

Details dress it up

Best friends are forever!

This traditional sweater is updated and designed in doll size. Cables and bobbles stand out against a flat purl background and suggest the look of appliqué. English shoulders streamline the contours of the cardigan because the front pieces are longer than the back ones. Exaggerated details, poufs, and big buttons emphasize the small fit. THIS PATTERN STARTS ON PAGE 88.

karate sweater

The deconstructed Karate Sweater's long front merges at the center back to shape the shoulder. Bypassing shoulder seams adds slouch and keeps the dojo stitch pattern continuous. Using extra-large needles softens the thickness created by the dojo stitch pattern. Exaggerated ribbing finishes the opening, creates contrast, and gives structure to this versatile design.

THIS PATTERN STARTS ON PAGE 91.

It's Good to Be Green!

pilot hat and flying gloves

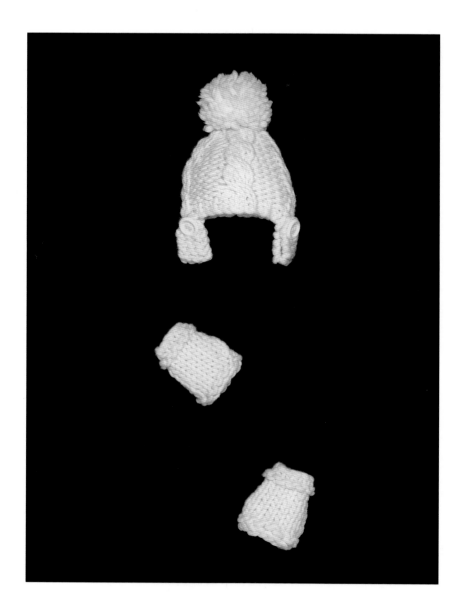

Fly first class with Twinkle's Pilot Hat!

Repeatedly decreasing on each stitch right next to the cable creates the hat's dome shape. Decreased stitches between cables become invisible, and eventually the hat looks like four interwoven cables. To make the flaps, pick up stitches from the edge. A pretty pom-pom tops it off. Keep your hands warm with the matching Flying Gloves. Wrapping yarn around the needle twice is a novel way to increase stitches and avoid bulkiness. To finish and give stability, use garter stitch. THIS PATTERN STARTS ON PAGE 94.

biker vest

Curves are crucial! To make hem curves that look like a shirttail, increase stitches frequently at both sides and ignore the irregular edges. After completing the body, clean up the edges by picking up the stitches along the outside edge and knitting in garter stitch all the way around. THIS PATTERN STARTS ON PAGE 98.

chelsea sweater

The lacy pattern in this cardigan creates an unstructured shape that adapts to your figure. A crochet trim around all the edges loosens the hem, creates bell sleeves, and ties it all together.

THIS PATTERN STARTS ON PAGE 96.

balthazar vest

Cap sleeves and a plunging V-neck send this vest right over the top. Simple shaping along the princess line creates a tailored yet come-hither look. THIS PATTERN STARTS ON PAGE 101.

tuxedo jacket

The Tuxedo Jacket, knit from top to bottom, is shaped like a trapezoid and is knit in a stretchy rib stitch. By folding the two sides up, the jacket has a short front with diagonal ribs and a long back with vertical ribs. Increasing by four stitches simultaneously fans out the rib at the center back. Knit the front and back as one piece and then pick up stitches to complete the sleeves. THIS PATTERN STARTS ON PAGE 99.

resort:
soft & sexy

The yarns, shapes, and colors in this chapter are perfect for traveling to the beaches of St. Tropez or St. Bart's. These resort designs will carry you effortlessly through any romantic getaway. Plus, packing is a breeze with light knits that not only look great but also never wrinkle!

LIGHT & CHUNKY These light Twinkle knits are a modern alternative to a blouse or a polo shirt. Knitted in silk and cotton, they make for versatile, comfortable tops. RELAXED & REFINED Look great in relaxed knits worn with eyelet skirts for brunch by the pool, or teamed with flowing silk dresses for an evening beach party. A SENSUOUS SILHOUETTE Ribbing at key areas, like the waist, makes a loose sweater sexy yet still comfortable. FLIRTY, FEMININE FINISHES Basic crochet edgings on necklines, hems, and pockets cast a sassy spell. MUTED MAGIC Warm-weather colors—tones of marine blue, citron yellow, and basic black—complement muted hues of mauve, lavender, and mint to give tight knits a softer touch.

seaside sweater

A romantic sweater with sex appeal, this design's tight ribbing is offset by a loose wave pattern. Ribbing at the waistline means the sweater will stretch and accommocate different body types. Alternating increases and decreases creates the wave pattern. The short-row technique emphasizes the sweater's bustline and adds to its flirty shape. THIS PATTERN STARTS ON PAGE 106.

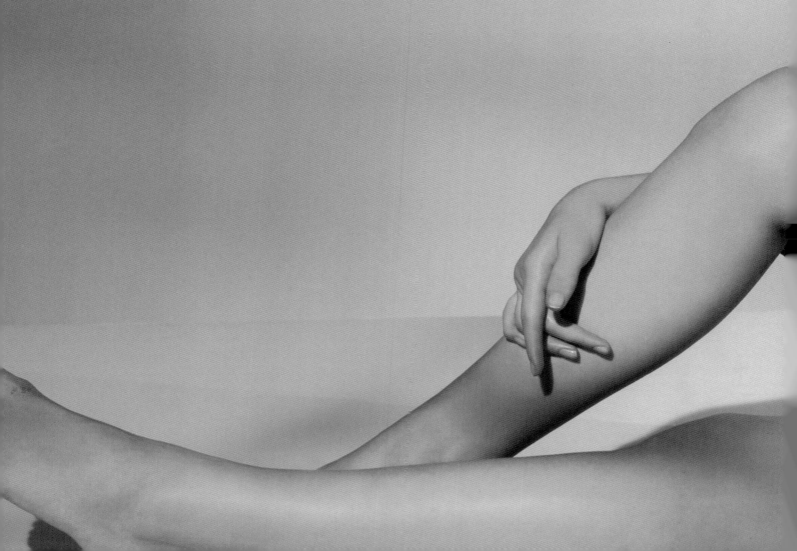

st. bart's mini

Knitting with circular needles all the way around means this dress is seamless, even when you turn down its funnel neck! Decreasing along the princess line instead of the sides creates the sexy, slim silhouette. Ribbing from the armholes to the back adds structure and pulls the design into shape. This mini is perfect for lounging by the pool under azure skies or going dancing after dark. THIS PATTERN STARTS ON PAGE 111.

coco jacket

All-over stockinette stitches make knitting this jacket easy for anyone! An alternative to the traditional rib or garter stitch for hems and openings, crochet adds feminine details to any sweater. Here, crochet graces the sleeve cuffs, hem, and pockets. Contrasting colors embolden its effect.

THIS PATTERN STARTS ON PAGE 109.

hamptons halter

When you layer chunky knits, the possibilities are endless! By knitting chunky yarn in an open-weave pattern, you create a fabric that's just right for warm weather. For a daytime look, light chunky knits work well with T-shirts. For cool evenings, pair them with a second sweater for style and warmth. This halter's wispy leaf pattern naturally forms a bikini camisole. Short rows emphasize the bustline, while ribbing accentuates the waist.

THIS PATTERN STARTS ON PAGE 112.

twiggy tunic

A cable-and-bud pattern graces the body and sleeves of this slim sweater. To make these details stand out, reverse stockinette stitch is used. Binding off loosely gives the sweater its off-the-shoulder neckline. Be true to Twiggy by making this sweater a size smaller than what you would typically wear. THIS PATTERN STARTS ON PAGE 119.

feather scarf

The modern alternative to a silk scarf, this knitted version is a must-have accessory for resort living! The airiness comes from the open stitchwork, which creates a featherlike fan when stitches are decreased along the center line. THIS PATTERN STARTS ON PAGE 122.

convertible cardigan

The most basic of Twinkle patterns, this cardigan is the perfect project for anybody who can knit and purl! Raglan sleeves give the sweater a fluid feel and the funnel neck adds versatility. Whether you wear it all buttoned up or open, you'll be ready for fun with this sweater in your weekend bag. THIS PATTERN STARTS ON PAGE 124.

night on the town:
daring & dramatic

People stop and stare when you arrive in knitwear! It's the new take on black tie. Make a glamorous entrance with daring and dramatic designs that go from day to evening effortlessly.

DRESSES ARE THE QUEENS OF THE NIGHT so crown them with knits! The mohair shrug, chunky bolero, and evening jacket will give your favorite dresses new life. DAZZLING DETAILS Go from simple to simply sensational, with exaggerated pom-poms, wide bell sleeves, lacy details, and more. SUPERSIZE IT! Knit mohair with extra-big needles, and your designs will be loose and sensuous. Big cables make shrunken sweaters sexy. STARTLING CONTRASTS Short with long, dark with light, knit with velvet—all spell glamour. SHIMMER & GLIMMER Smoky, muted colors, ranging from gray to charcoal to purple, are staples of nighttime dressing and will never go out of style. In loose weaves, they become translucent and enhance glittering evening fabrics. UPSWEPT HAIR Try a romantically disheveled look and pair it with clean makeup and super-smooth skin. Sparkly, shimmery eyes will ensure you stand out from the crowd. ACCESSORIZE YOUR ARRIVAL One simple strand of beads is utterly sophisticated.

Up Close and Personal

Creating the Incredible Skirt is an exciting and totally rewarding challenge. Bring a strong sense of color and your own personal touches to guarantee that no two skirts will ever be identical. THIS PATTERN STARTS ON PAGE 128.

incredible skirt

Looks can be deceiving! This skirt appears intricate but, in fact, it is made with the basic rib and stockinette stitches. Twinkle's modernized Fair Isle technique requires two yarns held together with needles that are one size larger than usual. Start with the two lightest yarns, interweaving one darker yarn sporadically and building up to a complete change. Repeat and continue from hem to waistline with four primary colors and six combinations. The color gets darker as the yarns gradually increase, and changing needles intensifies the effect. The transition from light to dark gives this skirt an airiness that dances and moves.

princess capelet

This fairy-tale jacket is knit entirely in seed stitch. Fashion the bell sleeves by decreasing frequently. Cuffing the sleeves adds sophistication and style. Chunky yarn emphasizes the flare, bell sleeves add drama, and pom-poms pull everything together with regal flair. **THIS PATTERN STARTS ON PAGE 130.**

mini bolero

Anyone who knows how to hold knitting needles can make the Mini
Bolero! This cropped cardigan is con-
structed with an all-over stockinette
stitch, set-in long sleeves, and a crochet picot edge. Knit it in quirky colors, and the jacket works as a stylish
accessory. THIS PATTERN STARTS ON
PAGE 132.

marilyn jacket

Tied with a satin ribbon and worn over a strapless cocktail dress, the Marilyn Jacket epitomizes old Hollywood. Two identical square pieces form the sweater's front and are connected by crossing from the shoulder to the back hem. The three-quarter length billowing sleeves add a touch of drama. Seaming sides and sleeves together gives the sweater its shape, while rib stitches at the front accentuate the trim. Good blocking sizes the sweater to seal the deal. THIS PATTERN STARTS ON PAGE 134.

evening shell

Twinkle's form-fitting Evening Shell has a small body with a big cable. The oversized cable looks even more dramatic because of the seed stitch background. Six more inches of knitting transforms the sweater into a dress. THIS PATTERN STARTS ON PAGE 136.

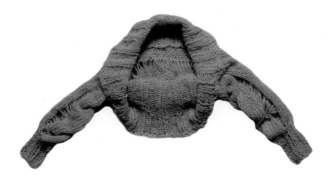

mohair shrug

Twinkle's take on mohair: Treat it like a chunky yarn! Bigger needles make stitches open up and give this sweater a luxurious feel. When binding off, drop two stitches and the sweater will assume an open, unraveling appearance. THIS PATTERN STARTS ON PAGE 138.

Never neglect the details

Picking up stitches on both ends creates cuffs; seaming one-third of each end makes the sweater opening and distinguishes the body; finally, a few runs of rib stitch blossom into the shawl collar.

shop the town: classic knits & great gifts

Shop till you drop! What could be better than spending an afternoon at Barneys or Bergdorf Goodman wearing Twinkle? Knitwear carries you effortlessly from the sophisticated stores of Madison Avenue to SoHo's swank boutiques. But don't let all this shopping stop you from making great gifts—surprise family and friends with your new knitting know-how and handmade creations.

STYLE 24/7 Cast a classic silhouette as you cruise city sidewalks with style and ease! These hoodies, turtlenecks, and cardigans make everyday a special occasion. SPARKLE IN TWINKLE Intarsia knits are the perfect, sporty alternative to ho-hum prints. Pair them with chunky accessories for signature Twinkle style! SHADES OF THE CITY Kelly green, icy blue, winter white, and classic coral are bright and beautiful enough to give you an energy boost. Basic black and mellow yellow complement the Twinkle girl's many moods. FRINGE IS FABULOUS There are so many ways to snip with scissors. Be adventurous and cut yarn shorter so it stands up. GIVE GIFTS OF LOVE Show them you care with handmade knitwear! Hats, scarves, and throws all make perfect presents. DAZZLE THEM WITH DETAILS Stripes are sublime and cables are divine. These adaptable details take you from shopping on Fifth Avenue and strolling in Central Park to sipping cocktails at the Carlyle! THE FRAME GAME Slide straight hair into a hat or collar and show off a fringe of beautiful bangs. Highlight pretty cheeks and eyes with warm, glistening makeup.

Short and cropped with three-quarter raglan sleeves, this hooded sweatshirt is knit in seed stitch. The entire sweater is one piece, pulled together by short rows along the neckline. Work up from the neckline to form the hood. A continuous rib band around the front opening completes this cozy piece, while extra-large buttons add style and sophistication. THIS PATTERN STARTS ON PAGE 142.

twinkle
hoodie

Lunch with your office crush? Team the
mellow yellow version with a corduroy
pencil skirt and black pumps.

aspen hat

Hit the slopes in style!

To make the Aspen Hat, knit ten rows for the band, decreasing at the corners to create the round shape, and overlap the end stitches. Garter stitch makes the band pop and extra-large buttons top it off! THIS PATTERN STARTS ON PAGE 145.

skating sweater

Cable merges into ribbing and then forms a seamless Peter Pan collar. English shoulders eliminate bulk with a longer front that slopes back. The sleeves are knit in one-by-one rib for an easy-going, vertical look. Wearers beware: The completed sweater will look extremely small and thick at first. The details come to life when you put it on and make it your own! THIS PATTERN STARTS ON PAGE 146.

rockefeller sweater

After knitting the body and sleeves, pick up stitches with a needle one size smaller than the one you have been using for the ribbing. The shawl collar is made by evenly picking up stitches along the neckline—short rows ensure that it lies flat. Patch pockets using the same pattern create continuity. THIS PATTERN STARTS ON PAGE 148.

magic shawl

4 strips of rib + 2 strips of cable = 1 Magic Cape. Ribs 1 and 2 are the opening band, rib 3 is the neckline, and rib 4 connects the two cables that form cape's shape. To keep the fringe on the right side, join the cables by working on wrong side. THIS PATTERN STARTS ON PAGE 151.

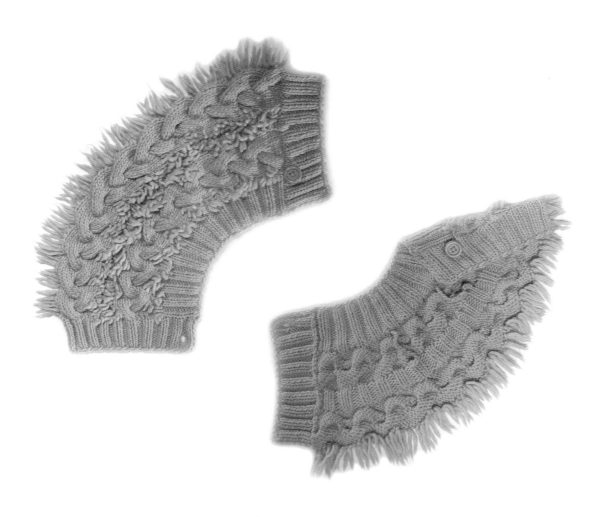

shopping tunic

This piece is knit completely with circular needles. Begin with four rounds of garter stitch at the hem and then keep on knitting. Turn it inside out when you're done knitting. Short rows create a smooth funnel neck, and decreases along the raglan seams make for narrow cap sleeves. THIS PATTERN STARTS ON PAGE 154.

Diamonds are a girl's best friend!

diamond scarf

Increasing and dropping stitches simultaneously create diagonal lines and form the shape. Larger needles make this scarf loose, soft, and stretchy. Wrap this Diamond Scarf around your neck and six feet of knitting magically grows to eight. THIS PATTERN STARTS ON PAGE 153.

twinkle tips and techniques

PREPARING FOR A PROJECT

First, take the time to build up your confidence and basic skills. Start every design by reviewing schematics, charts, and stitch patterns. Learn new approaches and hone your skills by experimenting with stitches on a small swatch. Many of my friends start projects, put them down, and then never finish them because they become too frustrated. Don't worry about mistakes—you can easily correct them, and they become part of the learning curve, another step on your road to success as a knitter.

When you complete a project and the design comes to life, you'll be showered with compliments and inspired to knit up something else.

With proper preparation, you will be ready to knit any of these thirty-one Twinkle patterns!

KNITTING IN THE ROUND

We love going in circles! Knitting with short, circular needles is modern and convenient. Circular needles fit into any hip handbag and travel everywhere. Since you don't need to join seams, you can knit all the way through without stopping.

Circular needles, available in many lengths, should be short enough to hold all your stitches without stretching them. I often use two circular needles to work on small necklines when the shortest circular needle is still too long. To accomplish this, divide the stitches evenly between two circular needles and knit with one circular needle at a time.

Although most patterns are written for straight, single-pointed needles, you can easily adjust the pattern for circular knitting.

What You Need

Pick up these basic knitting tools: knitting needles in various sizes, stitch markers, crochet needles in various sizes, darning needles, stitch holders, cable needles, and a needle gauge.

Here's a list of Twinkle tips for adapting a flat pattern to a circular knit design:
- The right side is always facing you.
- When working on multiple stitch patterns, take out the stitches that are outside the repeat.
- Reverse wrong side rows by reading the chart from right to left and making opposite stitches (for example, knit purl stitches and purl knit stitch).

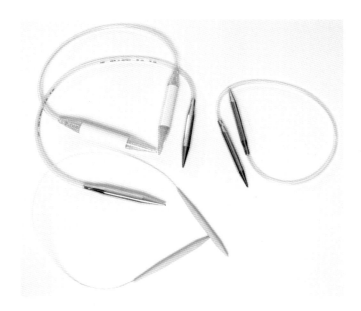

In the Round Circular needles are available in many lengths, sizes, and materials.

CHILL WITH CHUNKY YARN

Often, I design sweaters just because I fall in love with a particular yarn. It could be anything about the yarn—texture, color, or even the challenge of not knowing how to design with it. When I first learned to knit, I enjoyed working with chunky yarn because it is fast. Now, I have grown to appreciate its many facets and capabilities.

Yarns have personality. The bulkier and softer the yarn, the more difficult it is to achieve consistency in gauge. Its inconsistencies add an artistic element to the design. Bulky yarn inherently appears stiffer. Through knitting, I work the flaws of chunky yarn to its advantage. For quirky, tiny sweaters, I like to exaggerate the bulk and pile it up, making cable, bobbles, or anything three-dimensional. Conversely, with lacy, open-weave patterns, I love creating intricate sheer effects that are perfect for lingerie or deconstructed looks.

Be adventurous with chunkies! Remake a pattern you like in rainbow stripes instead of solids. Revitalize an old design by using a heavier yarn and a larger needle.

You will discover the joy of creating something unexpected from the familiar.

GO FOR IT WITH GAUGE

Gauge determines your design's measurements. Before knitting a sweater, make a swatch to ensure that you can achieve the correct gauge. If most of the garment is to be made in pattern stitch, make a swatch in the pattern stitch.

For chunkies, there are fewer than three stitches to an inch, so exact gauge is crucial. For accuracy, I suggest making a larger swatch and measuring from the middle. Make it match: If your gauge does not follow the example precisely, use a larger or smaller needle until it's right.

When working with circular needles, especially when you're doing stockinette stitch, purl is never used and the tension is tighter. Plan properly and allow yourself room for the difference.

From Chunky to Lacy Using a large needle for mohair can actually create a delicate lacy effect

KNITTING TECHNIQUES

Attaching Fringe

* Holding two or more strands together, fold strands in half. Insert crochet hook from back to front into garment and pull through doubled strands. Draw yarn ends through loop and pull tight. (illus. 1)

Basic Cables

* To make a knitted cable, you need to rearrange the order of the stitches in a row by using a cable needle.
* In this example, two stitches are slipped onto a cable needle. (illus. 1)
* The stitches on the cable needle are held in back of the work, while the next two stitches on the left-hand needle are knitted. (illus. 2)
* Then knit the stitches from the cable needle (illus. 3), which creates the twist.

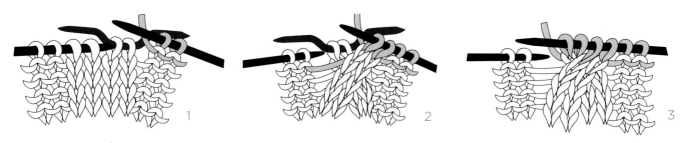

Crocheted Bind-Off

* Insert hook knitwise into first stitch on needle, yo and pull a loop through the stitch, allow stitch to drop off needle, ★insert hook knitwise into next st on needle, yo and pull a loop through both st on needle and st on hook, allow st to drop of needle; rep from ★.

Garter Stitch

Knit all rows.

Garter Stitch in the Round

Rnd 1: Knit
Rnd 2: Purl.

Joining Stitches

* On circular needles. (illus. 1)
* On double-pointed needles. (illus. 2)
* Make sure stitches are not twisted when you're joining.

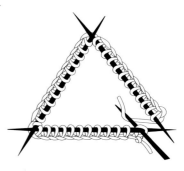

K1, P1 Rib
Row/Rnd 1: ★K1, p1; rep from ★.
Row/Rnd 2: Knit the knit sts and purl the purl sts.
Rep Row/Rnd 2 for pattern.

K2, P2 Rib
Row/Rnd 1: ★K2, p2; rep from ★.
Row/Rnd 2: Knit the knit sts and purl the purl sts.
Rep Row/Rnd 2 for pattern.

Making a Pom-Pom
* Cut two circles out of cardboard in a diameter slightly bigger than the size of the finished pom-pom.
* Cut a hole about half the size of the circles in the center. (illus. 1)
* Hold the two circles together and wind the yarn around the ring until the ring is completely covered. (illus. 2)
* Cut the yarn around the outside edge between the two circles. (illus. 3)
* Separate the two circles and tie the center into a firm knot.
* Remove the two circles and trim the pom-pom so it has a smooth edge. (illus. 4)

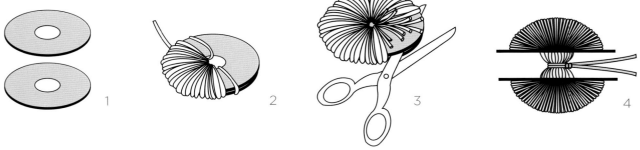

Making Buttonholes
* When you make a buttonhole with chunky yarn, binding off one stitch may be sufficient.
* For lighter-weight yarn, bind off more stitches, based on the button size. (illus. 1)
* On next row, use the e-loop method to cast on the same number of stitches that were bound off on the previous row. (illus. 2)

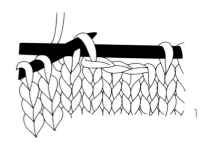

Making Bobbles

* To make a five-stitch bobble, knit into the front and the back of the same stitch twice (without slipping the stitches off the needle), then knit into the stitch once again. (illus. 1)
* Slip these five stitches to the left needle and work these five stitches in stockinette stitch (K on RS, P on WS) for a few rows. (illus. 2)
* Then with the RS facing, slip the stitches, one at a time, over the first stitch and off the needle. (illus. 3) Continue knitting the rest of the stitches on the left needle. (illus. 4)
* For chunky yarn, make bobbles by knitting just two or three stitches for two rows.
* For cruise yarn, make bobbles by knitting three to five stitches for two to three rows.

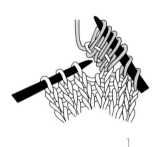   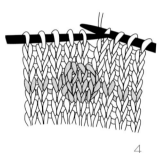

1   2   3   4

Making Patch Pockets

* When knitting with chunky yarns, pick up only half a stitch when you join pieces to avoid bulky seams. (illus. 1)
* Graft bound-off stitches onto live stitches by *inserting the needle inside the bound-off edge and then through two live stitches from the other side (knitwise for the first stitch and purlwise for the second)*. Repeat from *. (illus. 2)

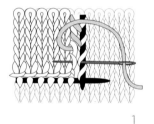 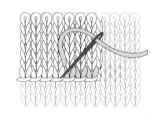

1   2

Markers

* Using markers is extremely important when you're knitting in the round.
  Used on the sides, center, front, and back, markers enable you to keep track of the beginning and the end.
* When joining, make sure stitches are not twisted around the needle.

Picking Up Stitches

* On vertical edges, pick up one stitch in between each stitch. (illus. 1)
* On horizontal edges, pick up one stitch in between each row. (illus. 2)

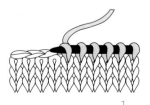 

1   2

Reverse Stockinette Stitch

When knitting in the round: Purl all rounds.

When knitting back and forth on straight needles: Purl right side rows, knit wrong side rows

Seaming/sewing

To seam finished pieces together, select from the techniques outlined below.

* To get started (illus. 1), insert needle from the back (WS) to the front (RS) in the corner stitches of each piece you want to sew together. Pull tightly to close the gap.
* For vertical seams on stockinette stitch (illus. 2), insert needle under the horizontal bar created by the edge stitch and the stitch next to it. Pull the yarn through and insert the needle into the corresponding bar on the opposite piece. Continue to work back and forth.
* For vertical seams on reverse stockinette stitch (illus. 3), insert needle into the loop created by the edge stitch. Pull the yarn through and insert the needle into the bottom loop of the corresponding stitch on the opposite piece. Continue to work back and forth.
* For horizontal seams on stockinette stitch (illus. 4), insert needle under a stitch inside the bound-off edge of one side. Pull yarn through and insert the needle under the corresponding stitch on the opposite side.
* For vertical to horizontal seams (illus. 5), insert needle under a stitch inside the bound-off edge of the vertical piece. Pull through and insert needle under the horizontal bars between the first and second stitches of the horizontal piece.

1

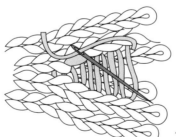

2

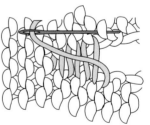

3

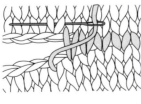

4

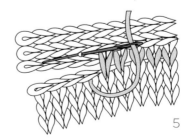

5

Seed Stitch

Row/Rnd 1: *K1, p1; rep from *.

Row/Rnd 2: Purl the knit sts and knit the purl sts.

Rep Row/Rnd 2 for pattern.

Short Rows

Short rows are made by working part of the way across a row, then turning and working back. However, in order to avoid a hole, you must "wrap" each stitch at the turning point. To wrap a stitch when the last stitch worked is a knit stitch: Knit to the turning point, slip next stitch onto right hand needle purlwise, turn work, bring yarn back between needles, slip stitch onto right hand needle, work next stitch on left hand needle (knit or purl—if a purl, you'll have to bring yarn foward between needles again to continue working).

All increases and decreases should be fully fashioned. In other words, whenever possible they should be made one stitch away from the edge of the fabric, or from the stitch markers.

Single Crochet

* Insert the crochet hook through the first stitch, YO, and pull the yarn through. (illus. 1)
* Insert hook through the second stitch and YO again (two loops in the hook). (illus. 2)
* YO and pull through both loops. (illus. 3)
* Insert hook through the next loop, YO (two loops), YO again, and pull through both loops on the hook. Repeat this step till the end of the row, then fasten by tying a slip knot.

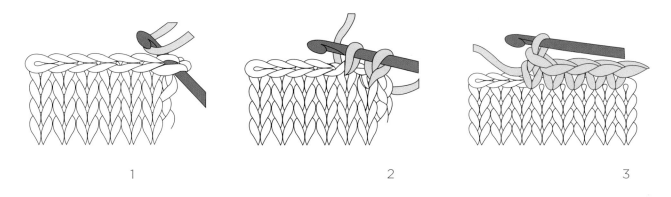

1   2   3

Sizing

Each pattern provides knitted measurements, which is what the garment should measure when laid out flat. You should choose your size (XS, S, M, or L) based on the following bust measurements.

XS	S	M	L	
30–31	32–33	34–35	36–37	inches
70–78.5	81–84	86.5–89	92–94	centimeters

Tasteful Tailoring

I adapted the English Shoulder technique to hand knitting. It's based on shorter seams that fall onto the upper back. The front piece is long and straight while the back piece is short and sloped. Front shoulder excess is folded on an angle toward the back so it meets the shoulder slope. Seam the front and back shoulder, binding off rows as you would a regular row-to-row seam. When you're done, the seam naturally falls onto the back, forming a smooth English Shoulder.

See the illustration (below) which shows a typical front and back piece before and after seaming an English Shoulder.

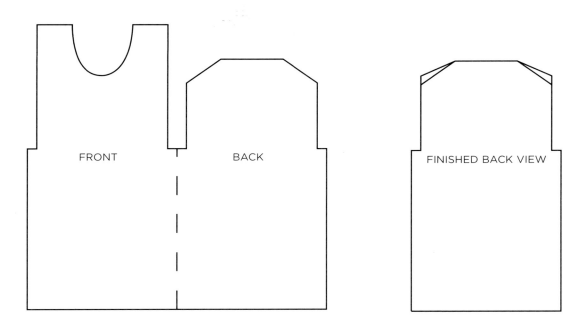

Three Needle Bind-Off

Hold pieces to be joined wrong sides together, with needles parallel to each other and pointing to the right.
* Insert right hand needle into the first stitch on the front needle and into the first stitch on the back needle, and knit these two stitches together. One stitch is now on the right hand needle.
* Knit together the next pair of stitches.
* Slip the first stitch on the right needle over the second stitch to bind it off.
* Repeat steps 2 and 3 until one stitch remains on needle. Fasten off.

Using Stitch Holders

Try using waste yarn as holder to keep from squeezing stitches onto a small stitch holder.

ABBREVIATIONS

R3L: Rib 3 left. Slip next st to cable needle and hold in front, knit 2nd st on left hand needle and leave on needle, purl first st on left hand needle and drop both sts off needle, knit st from cable needle.

C4R: Cable 4 right. Slip next 2 sts to cable needle and hold in back of work, k2, k2 from cable needle.

C6L: Cable 6 left. Slip next 3 sts to cable needle and hold in front of work, k3, k3 from cable needle.

C6R: Cable 6 right. Slip next 3 sts to cable needle and hold in back of work, k3, k3 from cable needle.

C8L: Cable 8 left. Slip next 4 sts to cable needle and hold in front of work, k4, k4 from cable needle.

C8R: Cable 8 right. Slip next 4 sts to cable needle and hold in back of work, k4, k4 from cable needle.

C10L: Cable 10 left. Slip next 5 sts to cable needle and hold in front of work, k5, k5 from cable needle.

C10R: Cable 10 right. Slip next 5 sts to cable needle and hold in back of work, k5, k5 from cable needle.

C12L: Cable 12 left. Slip next 6 sts to cable needle and hold in front of work, k6, k6 from cable needle.

C12R: Cable 12 right. Slip next 6 sts to cable needle and hold in back of work, k6, k6 from cable needle.

dbl tr: Double treble. Wrap yarn three times round hook, insert hook into st and pull up loop, (yo, pull through two loops) 4 times.

K: Knit.

M1: Make 1 increase.

MB: Make bobble. Into next st (k1, p1, k1, p1), turn, p4, turn, k4, turn, p4, turn, knit 4 together.

p2tog: Purl 2 sts together. Creates a right-leaning decrease on the knit side if the fabric.

P: Purl

pm: Place marker.

rem: Remain, remaining

rep: Repeat.

rnd: Round.

s2kp: Slip next 2 sts together as to knit, knit next st, pass 2 slipped sts over—creates a straight double decrease.

ssk: Slip, slip, knit. Slip next 2 sts one at a time as to knit, insert LH needle into both sts as to knit, knit sts together—creates a right-leaning decrease.

ssp: Slip, next 2 stitches one at a time as to knit, insert LH needle into both sts as to knit and slip back to LH needle; with RH needle, purl 2 sts together.

T2L: Twist 2 left. Knit through back loop into the 2nd st on left hand needle and leave st on needle, knit 2 together through back loop, slp;i both sts from needle.

T2R: Twist 2 right. Knit next 2 sts together, leaving sts on needle, knit first st, slip both sts from needle.

T2LP: Twist 2 left purl. Slip next st to cable needle and hold in front, p1, k1 from cable needle.

T2RP: Twist 2 right purl. Slip next st to cable needle and hold in back, k1, p1 from cable needle.

T3L: Twist 3 left. Slip next 2 sts onto cable needle and hold in front, p1, k2 from cable needle.

T3R: Twist 3 right. Slip next st onto cable needle and hold in back, k2, p1 from cable needle.

downtown

groovy sweater (dress)

KNITTED MEASUREMENTS
Bust: 30" (32½", 35") [76 (82.5, 89)cm]
Back length, including neckband: 29¾"
(30½", 31¼") [75.5 (77.5, 79)cm]

MATERIALS
6 (6, 7) skeins of Twinkle Handknits Soft
Chunky (100% merino wool; 83 yd/102 m
per 200 g skein) in Peach or Haze or 379 yd/
344 m of any super bulky weight yarn in
the color of your choice

US size 17 (12.75mm) and 19 (15mm) 24"
(61cm) circular needles

US size 17 (12.75mm) 16" (40.5cm) circular
needle

15 mm crochet hook

Stitch holders

GAUGE
9½ sts and 14½ rows = 6" (15cm) in St st
on size 19 needles.

NOTES
Sweater is knit in the round. Bodice and
sleeves are worked in reverse St st. The
sleeves are knit first.

SPECIAL STITCHES
C4R (Cable 4 right): Sl next 2sts to cable
needle and hold in back of work, K2, K2
from cn
MB (Make bobble): [K1, p1] 3 times, k1 in
one st (7sts made), then pass 2nd, 3rd, 4th,
5th, 6th, and 7th st over last st made
T2L (Twist 2 left): K through back loop
into 2nd st on left needle and leave st on
needle, k2tog through back loops, Sl both sts
from needle
T2R (Twist 2 right): K next 2 sts together,
leaving sts on needle, K 1st st again, Sl sts
off needle
T2LP (Twist 2 left purl): Sl next st to cn
and hold in front, P1, K1 from cn
T2RP (Twist 2 right purl): Sl next st to cn
and hold in back, K1, P1 from cn
T3L (Twist 3 left): Sl next 2 sts to cn and
hold in front, P1, K2, from cn
T3R (Twist 3 right): Sl next st to cn and
hold in back, K2, P1 from cn

LATTICE CABLES

(MULT OF 12)
RND 1 : K2, p8, *C4R, p8; rep from *,
k2.

RND 2: *K2, p8, K2; rep from *.

RND 3: *T3L, p6, T3R; rep from *.

RND 4: *P1, k2, p6, k2, p1; rep from *.

RND 5: *P1, T3L, p4, T3R, p1; rep
from *.

RND 6: *P2, k2, p4, k2, p2; rep from *.

RND 7: *P2, T3L, p2, T3R, p2; rep
from *.

RND 8: *P3, (K2, P2) twice, p1; rep
from *.

RND 9: *P3, T3L, T3R, p3; rep from *.

RND 10: *P4, k4, p4; rep from *.

LATTICE PATTERN

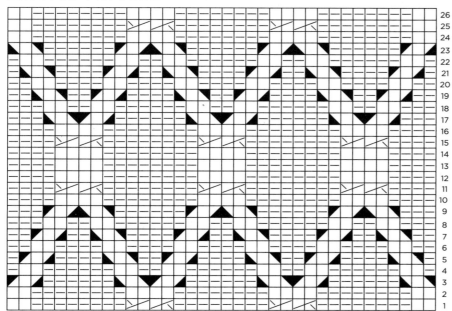

BOBBLE VINE PATTERN

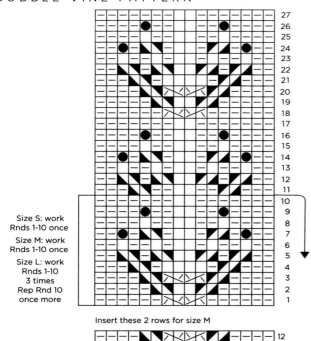

Size S: work
Rnds 1-10 once
Size M: work
Rnds 1-10 once
Size L: work
Rnds 1-10
3 times
Rep Rnd 10
once more

Insert these 2 rows for size M

= K on RS, P on WS

= P on RS, K on WS

= T2R

= T3L

= T3R

= T3L

RND 11: *P4, C4R, p4; rep from *.

RNDS 12-14: Rep Rnd 10.

RND 15: Rep Rnd 11.

RND 16: Rep Rnd 10.

RND 17: *P3, T3R, T3L, p3; rep from *.

RND 18: Rep Rnd 8.

RND 19: *P2, T3R, p2, T3L, p2; rep from *.

RND 20: Rep Rnd 6.

RND 21: *P1, T3R, p4, T3L, p1; rep from *.

RND 22: Rep Rnd 4.

RND 23: *T3R, p6, T3L; rep from *.

RND 24: Rep Rnd 2.

RND 25: Rep Rnd 1.

RND 24: Rep Rnd 2.

BOBBLE VINE
(PANEL OF 16)
SIZE SMALL

RND 1: P6, T2R, T2L, p6.

RND 2: P5, T2RP, k2, T2LP, p5.

RND 3: P4, T2RP, T2R, T2L, T2LP, p4.

RND 4: P3, T2RP, p1, k4, p1, T2LP, p3.

RND 5: P2, T2RP, p1, T2RP, k2, T2LP, p1, T2LP, p2.

RND 6: (P2, k1) two times, p1, k2, p1, (k1, p2) twice.

RND 7: P2, MB, p1, T2RP, p1, k2, p1, T2LP, p1, MB, p2.

RND 8: P4, k1, p2, k2, p2, k1, p4.

RND 9: P4, MB, p2, k2, p2, MB, p4.

RND 10: P7, k2, p7.

RND 11: P3, T2RP, p2, k2, p2, T2LP, p3.

RND 12: P2, T2RP, p1, T2RP, k2, T2LP, p1, T2LP, p2.

RND 13: (P2, k1) two times, p1, k2, p1, (k1, p2) twice.

RND 14: P2, MB, p1, T2RP, p1, k2, p1, T2LP, p1, MB, p2.

RND 15: P4, k1, p2, k2, p2, k1, p4.

RND 16: P4, MB, p2, k2, p2, MB, p4.

RND 17: Rep Rnd 10.

RNDS 18-27: Rep Rnds 1–10.

SIZE MEDIUM

RNDS 1-10: Same as Size Small.

RND 11: P5, T2RP, k2, T2LP, p5.

RND 12: P4, T2RP, T2R, T2L, T2LP, p4.

RNDS 13-19: Same as Size Small Rnds 11–17 above.

SIZE LARGE

RNDS 1-10: Same as Size Small above.

RNDS 11-20: Rep Rnds 1–10.

RND 21-30: Rep Rnds 1–10.

RND 31: Rep Rnd 10.

SLEEVES
(MAKE 2)
With smaller needles, CO 17 sts. Work k2, p2 rib for 4 rows, increasing 0 (2, 4) sts evenly spaced on last row—17 (19, 21) sts. Change to larger needles.

Work even in reverse St st, decreasing 1 st each side on Row 7, and increasing 1 st each side on Rows 19 and 31.

Work even until Sleeve measures 17". BO 2 sts at beg of next 2 rows. Place 15 (17, 19) sts on holder.

DRESS
With larger needles, CO 72 (76, 80) sts. Pm to indicate beg of rnd. Join, being careful not to twist sts.

Note: The Lattice Cable Pattern on sizes M and L will not match at side seams.

RND 1: P0 (1, 2), work Rnd 1 of Lattice Cable Pattern across next 36 sts, p0 (1, 2), pm to indicate left Underarm, p0 (1, 2), work Rnd 1 of Lattice Cable Pattern across next 36 sts, p0 (1, 2).

Cont in established Lattice Cable Pattern through Rnd 28. Change to smaller needles.

Work decreases and establish pattern as follows: Mark cables at either side of center front.

Begin k2, p2 rib, purling 2 sts tog 28 times evenly spaced in reverse St st portions of fabric AT THE SAME TIME, setting up ribbing so that marked cables have 2 knit (rib) stitches above them, and (p2, k2, p2) in between—44 (48, 52) sts. Work k2, p2 rib as established for a total of 10 rnds.

Change to larger needles and reverse St st.

RND 1: P1, m1, p2 (3, 4), work Bobble Vine Pattern across next 16 sts, p2 (3, 4), m1, pm, purl across Back sts to last 2 sts, p1.

Work even 5 rnds. Inc 1 st each side of marker once—50 (54, 58) sts. Work even until 10 rnds above ribbing, ending last rnd 2 sts before end of rnd.

DIVIDE BODY
Bind off 4 sts, pattern across next 22 (24, 26) Front sts, bind off next 4 sts, purl across 20 (22, 24) Back sts.

JOIN SLEEVES
Pm, purl across 15 (17, 19) Sleeve sts, pm, work in pattern across front sts, pm, purl across 15 (17, 19) Sleeve sts, pm, purl across back sts—72 (80, 88) sts.

Working reverse St st in the round (purl all rnds), work even 3 rnds. Next rnd (Dec Rnd): *P1, p2tog, purl to 3 sts before marker, p2tog, p1; rep from * around. Rep Dec Rnd every 3rd rnd 4 (5, 6) more times—32 sts.

FRONT NECK SHAPING
Purl across Sleeve sts, pattern across 12 front sts and place on holder, purl to end of rnd, purl across Left Sleeve sts, turn.

Next row: BO 2 sts at neck edge, knit to marker, sl marker, k1, ssk, knit to 3 sts before next marker, k2tog, knit to end of row. BO 2 sts at beg of next row, purl to end—12 sts rem.

With shorter circular needle, knit 28 sts around Neck, including 12 Back Neck and 12 Front Neck sts from holder. Work 3 rnds in k2, p2 rib, arranging ribbing so that 2 knit (rib) sts are above Center Front knit sts. Bind off loosely.

FINISHING
Sew Sleeve seams. Weave Underarm seams. Weave in ends.

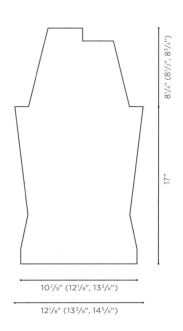

8¹/₄" (8¹/₂", 8³/₄")

17"

10⁷/₈" (12¹/₈", 13³/₈")

12¹/₈" (13³/₈", 14⁵/₈")

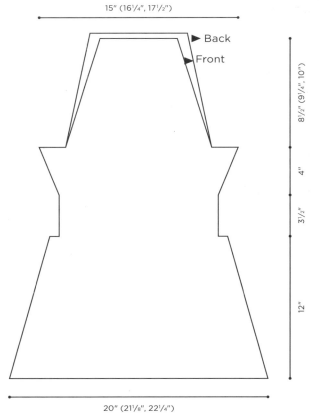

15" (16¹/₄", 17¹/₂")

► Back

► Front

8¹/₂" (9¹/₄", 10")

4"

3¹/₂"

12"

20" (21¹/₈", 22¹/₄")

12" (13", 14")

best friend cardigan

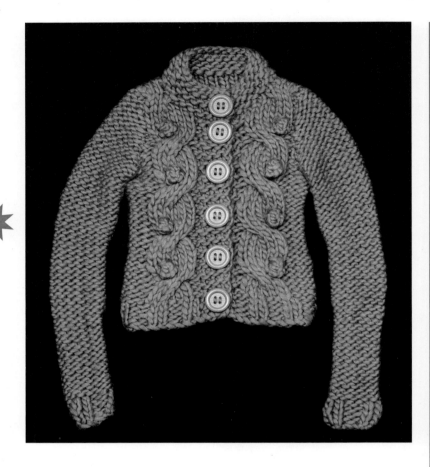

KNITTED MEASUREMENTS
Bust: 28" (30½", 33") [71 (78, 84)cm]
Back Length: 20" (20½", 21") [51 (52, 53)cm]

MATERIALS
4 (5, 5) skeins of Twinkle Handknits Soft Chunky (100% merino wool; 83 yd/77 m per 200 g ball) in French Grey *or* 240 yd/ 247 m of any super bulky weight yarn

US size 19 (15mm) 24" (61cm) circular needles

Stitch holders

Stitch markers

Six 1¾" (4.5cm) buttons

GAUGE
9½ sts and 14½ rows = 6" (15cm) in St st on size 19 needles

NOTES
This sweater is worked back and forth on a circular needle. Body is worked in one piece to the underarm.
Body and sleeves are worked in reverse St st. Keep first and last 4 sts in garter stitch (knit every row).

SPECIAL STITCHES
C6L (Cable 6 left): Slip next 3 sts to cable needle and hold in front of work, k3, k3 from cable needle
C6R (Cable 6 right): Slip next 3 sts to cable needle and hold in back of work, k3, k3 from cable needle
MB (Make bobble): [K1, p1] 3 times, k1 in one st (7sts made in one st), then pass 2nd, 3rd, 4th, 5th, 6th, and 7th st over last st made
SSK: Slip next 2 sts one at a time as to knit, insert LH needle into both sts as to knit and slip back to LH needle; with RH needle, purl 2 sts together

RIGHT CABLE

ROWS 1 AND 3 (RS): P1, k6, p2.

ROW 2 AND ALL WS ROWS: K2, p6, k1.

ROW 5: P1, C6R, p2.

ROW 7: P1, k4, MB, k1, p2.

ROW 8: K2, p6, k1.

Rep Rows 1–8.

LEFT CABLE

ROWS 1 AND 3 (RS): P2, k6, p1.

ROW 2 AND ALL WS ROWS: K1, p6, k2.

ROW 5: P2, C6L, p1.

ROW 7: P2, k1, MB, k4, p1.

ROW 8: K1, p6, k2.

Rep Rows 1–8.

BODY

Cast on 48 (52, 56) sts.

ROW 1 (RS): K4, ★k2, p2; rep from ★ to last 4 sts, k4.

ROW 2: K4, work established k2, p2 rib across next 40 (44, 48) sts, k4.

ROW 3 (BUTTONHOLE ROW): K2, yo, k2tog, rib to last 4 sts, k4.

ROW 4: K4, work established rib over next 9 (10, 11) sts, pm, cont in rib across 22 (24, 26) sts, pm, cont in rib across next 9 (10, 11) sts, k4.

ROW 5 (ESTABLISH PATTERN AND INC ROW): K4, work Right Cable across next 9 sts, p0 (1, 2), m1, p1, m1, purl to 1 st before marker, m1, p1, m1, p0 (1, 2), work Left Cable across next 9 sts, k4—52 (56, 60).

Cont in established patterns, making buttonholes every 8 rows.

AT THE SAME TIME shape body as follows: Work even 6 rows. Next row (Dec Row): ★Work to 2 sts before marker, p2tog, ssp; rep from ★ once, work to end.

Work even 9 rows, then repeat Inc Row—52 (56, 60) sts. Work even until 3 full repeats of cable pattern are complete. Sweater measures approx 11½" (29cm) from beginning.

RIGHT CABLE PATTERN

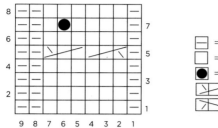

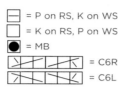

= P on RS, K on WS

= K on RS, P on WS

= MB

= C6R

= C6L

LEFT CABLE PATTERN

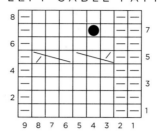

DIVIDE BODY

Maintaining pattern, work 13 (14, 15) Right Front sts, place these sts on holder, bind off 2 sts, purl 22 (24, 26) Back sts, place remaining 15 (16, 17) Underarm and Left Front sts on holder. On Back sts only, work 4 rows even. Next row (Dec Row): K1, ssk, k to last 3 sts, k2tog, k1—20 (22, 24) sts. Work even until Armhole measures 5" (5⅜", 5¾") [13 (13.5, 14.5)cm].

SHOULDER SHAPING

Dec 1 st each side every row 5 (6, 7) times—10 sts. Place remaining Back Neck sts on holder.

Place Right Front sts on needle. Beg with a WS row, work 3 rows even. Next row (Dec Row): Work to last 3 sts, p2tog, p1. Work even until four full repeats of cable pattern are complete, ending with a WS row.

NECK SHAPING

BO 4 sts at Neck edge once, 2 sts once, and 1 st once—5 (6, 7) sts. Work even until Right Front Armhole measures 6½" (7", 7 ½") [16.5 (18, 19)cm]. Bind off.

Place Underarm and Left Front sts on needle. With RS facing, BO 2 sts, work to end. Work 3 rows even. Next row (Dec Row): P1, ssp, work to end. Work even until 4 full repeats of cable pattern are complete, ending with a WS row. Work 1 row even.

NECK SHAPING

BO 4 sts at Neck edge once, 2 sts once, and 1 st one time—5 (6, 7) sts. Work even until Left Front Armhole measures 6½" (7", 7½")[16.5 (18, 19)cm]. Bind off.

SLEEVES
(MAKE 2)
CO 13 (15, 17) sts.

ROW 1: K1, *p1, k1; rep from *. Work 3 more rows in k1, p1 rib as established.

Change to reverse St st and work even 14 rows. Next row (Inc Row): P1, m1, purl to last st, m1, p1. Work even 11 rows, then rep Inc Row—17 (19, 21) sts. Work even until Sleeve measures 18" (46cm) from beg.

CAP SHAPING

BO 1 st at beg of next 10 rows. BO rem 7 (9, 11) sts.

FINISHING
Sew Shoulder seams.

With RS facing and larger needles, pick up 10 (11, 12) sts along Right Front Neck edge, 10 sts across Back, and 10 (11, 12) sts along Left Front Neck edge—30 (32, 34) sts. Knit 5 rows. Bind off loosely.

Set in Sleeves and sew Sleeve seams. Weave in ends.

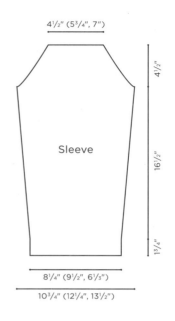

4½" (5¾", 7")

4½"

Sleeve

16½"

1¾"

8¼" (9½", 6⅓")

10¾" (12¼", 13½")

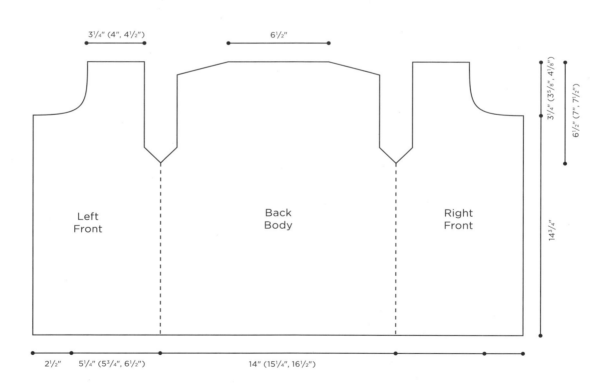

3¼" (4", 4½")

6½"

3¼" (3⅝", 4⅛")

6½" (7", 7½")

Left
Front

Back
Body

Right
Front

14¾"

2½"   5¼" (5¾", 6½")   14" (15¼", 16½")

karate sweater

KNITTED MEASUREMENTS
Bust: 30" (33", 33") [76 (84, 84)cm]
Length (excluding collar): 30¾" (31½",
32¼") [78.1 (80, 81.9)cm]

MATERIALS
6 (7, 8) skeins of Twinkle Handknits Soft
Chunky (100% merino wool; 83 yd/77 m
per 200 g skein) in Asparagus or 501¼ yd/
456m of any super bulky weight yarn in the
color of your choice

US size 36 (19mm) 29" (73.5cm) circular
needle

US size 17 (12.75mm) 29" (73.5cm) circular
needle

Size N (10mm) crochet hook

One 2" (5cm) button

Stitch holders

GAUGE
8 sts and 10½ rows = 6" (15cm) in Dojo
Stitch on size 36 needles

NOTES
This sweater is worked back and forth on a
circular needle. The body is knit in one
piece to armholes.

SPECIAL STITCHES
k2tog: K2 together
SSK: Slip, slip, K 2 together
yo: Yarn over

DOJO STITCH
(MULT OF 4)
ROW 1 (RS): *K2, yo, ssk; rep from *.

ROW 2: *P2, yo, p2tog; rep from *.

Rep Rows 1–2.

DOJO PATTERN

☐ = K on RS, P on WS
◯ = yo
⟍ = SSK
⟋ = K2tog

BODY
With larger needle, CO 40 (44, 44) sts. Work in Dojo Stitch until
you have completed 32 rows. Piece measures approx 18" (46cm).

DIVIDE FOR ARMHOLES
Work in pattern across 8 Right Front sts, place these sts on a
holder, BO next 4 sts, work in pattern across 16 (20, 20) Back
sts, place rem 12 sts on holder for Underarm and Left Front.

Working on Back stitches only, work even for 11 (13, 15) more
rows. Back measures approximately 24¾" (25½", 26¼") [63 (65,
67)cm]. Bind off.

RIGHT FRONT
Place Right Front sts on larger needle. Beg with WS, work even
for 19 (22, 25) rows. Right Front measures approx 29" (30½", 32")
[73.5 (77.5, 81)cm]. Place sts on smaller needle as holder.

LEFT FRONT
Place 12 Underarm and Left Front sts on larger needle. With RS
facing, join yarn, BO 4 sts, work in pattern to end of row. Work
even in pattern on 8 sts until Left Front measures same as Right
Front. Holding needle with Right Front sts parallel to Left Front sts,
work 3-needle bind-off for Center Back seam.

SLEEVES

(MAKE 2)

CO 16 (18, 20) sts.

Sizes S and L: Work even in the Dojo Stitch until Sleeve measures 25" (63.5cm).

Size M only: K1, work in the Dojo Stitch across next 16 sts, k1. Cont working in pattern, keeping first and last sts in St st, until Sleeve measures 25" (63.5cm).

All sizes: Bind off.

FINISHING

Pin Center Back seam to center point of 16 (20, 20) Back stitches and sew. Fold Sleeve in half and set into Armhole. Sew Sleeve seam.

BANDS

With smaller needles and RS facing, join yarn at lower Right Front Edge and pick up 104 (110, 116) sts on Front edge, around Neck, and down Left Front edge.

ROW 1 (WS): P3, *k2, p2; rep from *, p1.

ROW 2: Knit the knit sts and purl the purl sts.

Cont in established rib pattern for 7 (7, 11) more rows.

Buttonhole row: K3, *p2, k2; rep from * 4 times, yo, p2tog, cont in established k2, p2 rib to end. Work 2 rows even. BO in rib.

BELT

With smaller needle, CO 4 sts. Knit 170 rows. Stretch belt lengthwise and block.

BELT LOOPS

Make two 2" (5cm) crochet chains and sew one on each side 7" (18cm) below Armhole bind-offs.

Sew button opposite buttonholes. Weave in ends.

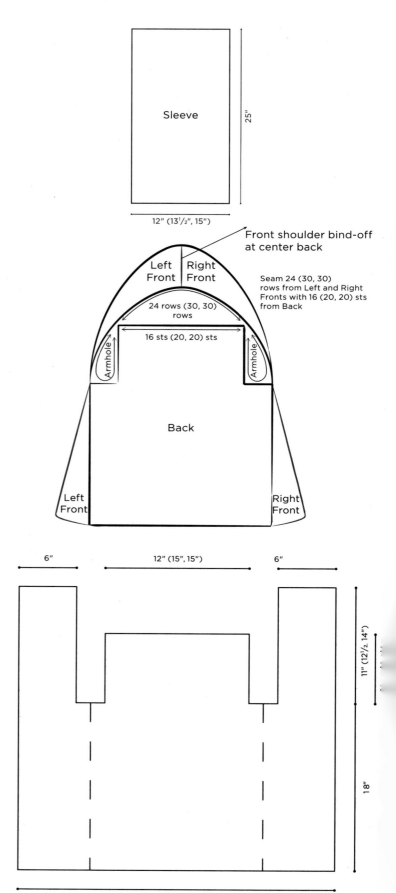

pilot hat

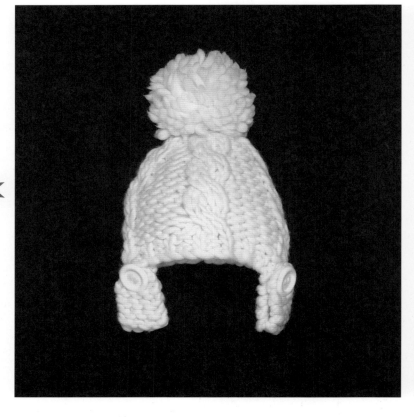

MATERIALS
1 skein of Twinkle Handknits Soft Chunky (100% merino wool; 83 yd/77 m per 200 g skein) in Peacock Blue or White *or* 66 yd/ 62 m of any super bulky weight yarn in the color of your choice

US size 19 (15mm) 16" (40.5cm) circular knitting needles

One set of 4 or 5 US size 19 (15mm) double-pointed needles

Two 1½" (4cm) buttons

GAUGE
8½ sts and 10½ rows = 5" (13cm) in Pilot Cable Pattern on size 19 needles

SPECIAL STITCHES
C4R (Cable 4 right): Slip next 2 sts to cable needle and hold in back of work, k2, k2 from cable needle

PILOT CABLE
(MULT OF 8)
RNDS 1–2: *K4, p4; rep from *.

RND 3: *C4R, p4; rep from *.

RND 4: *K4, p4; rep from *.

Rep Rnds 1–4.

PILOT CABLE PATTERN

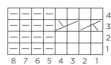

☐ = K on RS, P on WS

⊟ = P on RS, K on WS

⧖ = C4R

HAT
CO 32 sts. Pm to indicate beginning of rnd. Join, being careful not to twist sts.

RNDS 1–2: *K1, p1; rep from *.

Beg Pilot Cable Pattern. Work even for 7 rnds. On Rnd 8, begin decreases as follows:

RND 8: *K4, p2, p2tog; rep from *—28 sts.

RND 10: *K4, p1, p2tog; rep from *—24 sts.

RND 12: *K4, p2tog; rep from *—20 sts.

RND 14: *K3, ssk; rep from *—16 sts.

Work two more rnds, ending with Rnd 4 of Cable Pattern.

Cut yarn, thread through remaining sts, and pull tight. Weave in ends.

STRAPS
With RS facing, from cast-on edge pick up 4 sts directly under one cable. Knit 20 rows.

ROW 21: K2, yo, k2tog.

ROW 22: Knit.

ROW 23: K2tog, k2—3 sts.

Bind off.

Make second Strap on opposite side of Hat.

Sew buttons 1" (2.5cm) from edge of hat.

Fold Strap up and button.

Make a pom-pom 4" (10cm) in diameter (see page 75) and sew to top of Hat.

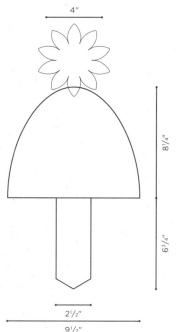

flying gloves

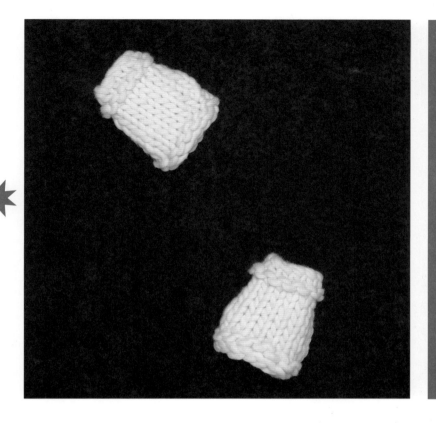

ONE SIZE

MATERIALS
1 skein of Twinkle Handknits Soft Chunky (100% merino wool; 83 yd/77 m per 200 g skein) in White *or* in any super bulky weight yarn in the color of your choice

US size 19 (15mm) knitting needles

Stitch holders

Stitch marker

GAUGE
9½ sts and 14½ rows = 6" (15cm) in St st on size 19 needles

GLOVES
(MAKE 2)
CO 11 sts.

ROWS 1–2: Knit.

ROW 3: K1, knit next st, wrapping yarn twice around needle, knit to end.

ROW 4: P9, (k1, p1) into double-wrapped stitch, p1—12 sts.

ROW 5: Knit.

ROW 6: P10, purl next st, wrapping yarn twice around needle, p1.

ROW 7: K1, (k1, p1) into double-wrapped stitch, knit to end—13 sts.

ROW 8: Purl.

ROW 9: BO 1, knit to end.

ROW 10: BO 1, knit to end.

ROWS 11–12: Knit.

Bind off. Sew side seam. Weave in ends.

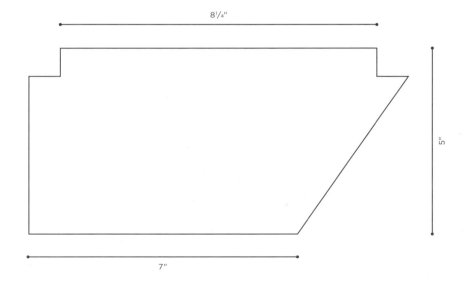

8¼"

5"

7"

chelsea sweater

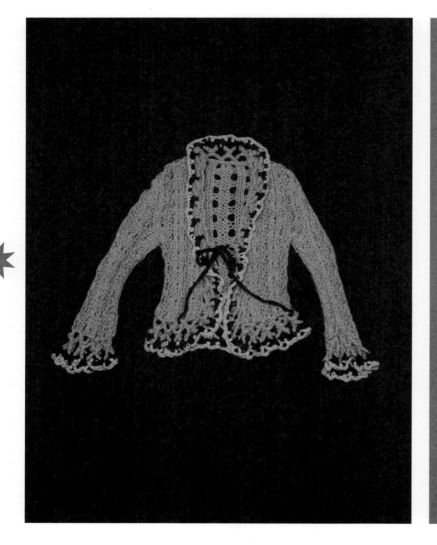

CHELSEA STITCH
(MULT OF 6 + 2)
ROW 1: K1, k1, yo, ssk, k2tog, yo, k1; rep from *, k1.

CHELSEA PATTERN

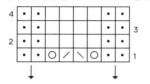

Repeat between arrows

• = K on RS, K on WS
○ = yo
\ = SSK
/ = K2tog
☐ = K on RS, P on WS

ROW 2: K1, *k1, p4, k1; rep from *, k1.

ROW 3: Knit.

ROW 4: K1, *k1, p4, k1; rep from *, k1.

Rep Rows 1–4.

BODY
With A, cast on 50 (56, 62, 68) sts. Work in Chelsea Stitch until 20 rows are complete. Piece measures approx 8" (20cm).

DIVIDE FOR ARMHOLES
Work in pattern across 12 (15, 15, 18) Right Front sts, m1, k1, place these 14 (17, 17, 20) sts on a holder, k1, m1, work in pattern across 22 (22, 28, 28) Back sts, m1, k1, place remaining 13 (16, 16, 19) Left

Front sts on holder.

Working on Back sts only, work even for 19 (21, 23, 25) more rows. Back measures approximately 16" (16¾", 17½", 18¼") [41 (42.5, 44, 46)cm].

K9 (9, 11, 11) Right Shoulder sts, place on holder, bind off next 8 (8, 10, 10) Back Neck sts, k 9 (9, 11, 11) Left Shoulder sts, place on holder.

RIGHT FRONT
Place Right Front sts on needle. Beg with wrong side, work even until Front measures same as Back to Shoulders. Holding needle parallel with holder containing 9 (9, 11, 11) Right Shoulder sts, work 3-needle bind-off.

Note: There are a different number of stitches front and back. Work an occasional two Front stitches together with a single Back stitch to ease in the difference.

LEFT FRONT

Place Left Front sts on needle. With RS facing, join yarn, m1, knit to end of row. Work as for Right Front to Shoulder shaping.

Bind off stitches with Back Left Shoulder sts as for Right Front.

SLEEVE

(MAKE 2)

With A, cast on 20 (23, 26, 29) sts. Row 1 (right side): Knit 0 (2, 0, 2), work in Chelsea Pattern across next 20 (20, 26, 26) sts, knit 0 (1, 0, 1).

ROW 2: Purl 0 (1, 0, 1), work in Chelsea Pattern across next 20 (20, 26, 26) sts, purl 0 (2, 0, 2). Work even in established pattern for 26 more rows.

CAP SHAPING

BO 3 sts at beg of next 2 rows—14 (14, 20, 20) sts. Work even 6 (8, 10, 12) more rows. Bind off.

FINISHING

Set in Sleeves, easing in excess around corners.

Sew Sleeve seams.

SLEEVE EDGINGS

With RS facing and crochet hook, join A and work edging as follows:

RND 1: Ch 1, *ch 5, sc in cast-on edge; rep from * 6 (7, 8, 9) times, end with sl st in beg ch-1.

RND 2: Sl st in next 2 ch, *sc in next ch-5 sp, ch 6; rep from *, end with sl st in sc. End off A.

RND 3: With B, sc in any ch-6 sp, ch 7, *sc in next ch-6 sp, ch 7; rep from *, end with sl st in sc. End off B.

RND 4: With C, join yarn in any ch-7 sp, in same sp (sc, ch 3, sc), ch 3, *in next ch-7 sp (sc, ch 3, sc), ch 3; rep from *, end with sl st in beg sc. End off C.

Repeat for second Sleeve.

BODY EDGING

With RS facing and crochet hook, with A, work around entire outside edge of sweater as for Sleeves, working a total of 46 (50, 55, 59) loops around.

TIES

With B, crochet two chains 20" (51cm) long. Sew to first row of edgings 8" (20cm) from cast-on edge. Weave in ends.

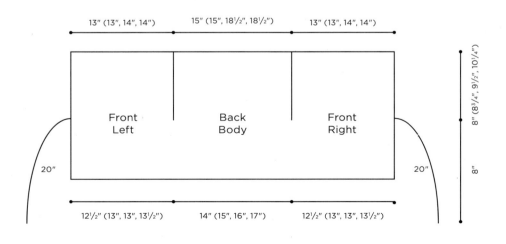

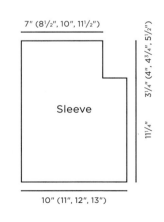

biker vest

SIZES S (M, L)

KNITTED MEASUREMENTS
Bust: 29", (30", 31") [74 (76, 79)cm]
Back Length: 15½", (16", 16½") [39 (41, 42)cm]

MATERIALS
6 (6, 7) skeins of Twinkle Handknits Cruise (70% silk, 30% cotton; 120 yd/112 m per 50 g skein) in Grey or Black or 473 yd/443 m of any super bulky weight yarn in the color of your choice

US size 15 (10mm) 24" (61cm) circular needle

Stitch holders

GAUGE
Holding 4 strands together, 11 sts and 18½ rows = 5" (13cm) in Lace Pattern on size 15 needles
9 sts = 4" (10cm) in garter stitch

NOTES
This sweater is worked back and forth on a circular needle. Body is worked in one piece to the underarm.
Always work first and last sts at front edges in St st (knit on RS, purl on WS). Bring new sts into pattern as stitch count changes.

SPECIAL STITCHES
S2KP: Sl 2 sts together as if to k, k1, p2sso (pass 2 sl sts over)
yo : Yarn over

BIKER LACE PATTERN
(MULT OF 6 + 3)
ROW 1 (WS): *P3, k3; rep from *, p3.

ROW 2: K3, *yo, s2kp yo, k3; rep from *.

ROW 3: *K3, p3; rep from *, k3.

ROW 4: Yo, s2kp, yo, *K3, yo, s2kp, yo; rep from *.

Rep Rows 1–4.

LACE PATTERN

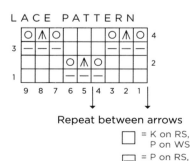

Repeat between arrows

▢ = K on RS, P on WS

⊟ = P on RS, K on WS

◯ = yo

◺ = S2KP

BODY
CO 41 (47, 53) sts.

ROW 1 (WS): P1, work Row 1 of Lace Pattern to last st, p1.

ROW 2: CO 3 sts, work established Lace Pattern to end, k1.

ROWS 3–7: Rep Row 2, keeping first and last sts in St st—59 (65, 71) sts after Row 7 is complete. Work even until 6 repeats of Lace Pattern have been completed. Piece measures approx 6½" (16.5cm).

DIVIDE BODY
BO 2 sts at beg of next row, k10 (11, 13), place these Right Front sts on holder, BO next 4 sts, k27 (31, 33) Back sts, place rem 16 (17, 19) Left Front sts on holder.

BACK
On Back sts only, beg with a WS row, BO 1 st at beg of next 4 rows—23 (27, 29) sts.

Work even until Armhole measures 7" (7½", 8") [18 (19, 20)cm]. BO 5 (6, 7) sts at beg of next 2 rows. Place remaining 13 (15, 15) Back Neck sts on holder.

RIGHT FRONT
Place Right Front sts on needle. Beg with a WS row, BO 1 st at Armhole edge 1 time. AT THE SAME TIME bind off 2 sts at Neck edge once and 1 st 2 (2, 3) times—5 (6, 7) sts rem. Work even until Armhole measures same as Back. Bind off.

LEFT FRONT
Place Left Front sts on needle. Beg with a right side row, BO 4 sts at Armhole edge, work to end. At Neck edge, BO 2 sts 2 times and 1 st 2 (2, 3) times. AT THE SAME TIME at Armhole edge BO 1 st 1

time—5 (6, 7) sts rem. Work even until Armhole measures same as Back. Bind off.

FINISHING

Sew Shoulder seams. With RS facing, pick up and knit 140 (143, 146, 149) sts around entire outside edge of vest, including 13 (15, 15) Back Neck sts from holder. Place marker for beg of rnd. Work 5 rows garter st (purl 1 round, knit 1 round). BO loosely.

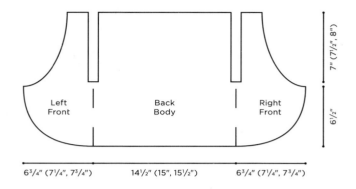

Left Front

Back Body

Right Front

7" (7½", 8")

6½"

6¾" (7¼", 7¾")   14½" (15", 15½")   6¾" (7¼", 7¾")

tuxedo jacket

SIZES S (M, L)

KNITTED MEASUREMENTS
Bust: 16½" (18½", 20½")
Length: 27" (68.5cm)

MATERIALS
7 (8, 9) skeins of Twinkle Handknits Soft Chunky (100% merino wool; 83 yd/77 m per 200 g skein) in White or 568 yd or 518 m of any super bulky weight yarn in the color of your choice

US size 19 (15 mm) 32" (89cm) circular needle

US size 19 (15 mm) 16" (40.5cm) circular needle for sleeves

Stitch markers

Stitch holders

GAUGES
9½ sts and 14½ rows = 6" (15cm) in St st on size 19 needles
8 sts and 9 rows = 4" (10cm) in k2, p2 rib, relaxed

NOTES
Sweater is knit from the top down. Circular needles are used to accommodate the large number of stitches, and to fit around armhole opening when knitting sleeves from the top down. Use (k2tog) or (p2tog) decreases as necessary to keep all decreases in pattern stitch.

SPECIAL STITCHES
C10L (Cable 10 left): Slip next 5 sts to cable needle and hold in front of work, k5, k5 from cable neddle
C10R (Cable 10 right): Slip next 5 sts to cable needle and hold in back of work, k5, k5 from cable needle

BODY

CO 100 (108, 116) sts.

ROW 1 (RS): K3, *p2, k2; rep from * to last st, k1.

Cont in established k2, p2 rib until 18 rows are complete.

DIVIDE FOR ARMHOLES

Mark center Back rib. Cont in rib pattern, work 17 (18, 19) Left Front sts, work next 23 (25, 27) Sleeve sts and place on holder, dec 1, pattern to center rib, (yo, k1, yo) into next st, (k1, yo, k1) into next st [4 sts increased], pattern until 42 (45, 48) sts rem, dec 1, place next 23 (25, 27) Sleeve sts on holder, pattern across remaining 17 (18, 19) Right Front sts—56 (60, 64) sts.

Cont in established k2, p2 rib, working into back of yo from previous row and inc 4 sts at center Back every 10 rows 3 more times—68 (72, 76) sts. Work even until 60 rows are complete. Sweater measures approx 27" (68.5cm). Bind off.

SLEEVE
(MAKE 2)

Place 23 (25, 27) Sleeve sts on smaller circular needle. Working back and forth in St st, work even 12 rows. Next row (Dec Row): K1, ssk, knit to last 3 sts, k2tog, k1. Rep Dec Row every 10th row 2 times—17 (19, 21) sts. Work even until Sleeve measures 15½" (39cm) from Underarm. Change to k2, p2 rib and work 14 rows. Bind off.

CABLE BAND

CO 17 sts. Work 2 (2, 0) rows even in St st.

Begin cable:

ROWS 1, 5, AND 7 (RS): Knit.

ROW 2 AND ALL WS ROWS: Purl.

ROW 3: K1, C10R, k6.

ROW 9: K6, C10L, k1.

ROWS 11 AND 13: Knit.

ROW 14: Knit.

Rep Rows 1–6 (8, 12).

Bind off.

FINISHING

On cast-on edge, place marker 27 (29, 31) sts in from each side. Pin cable band along next 17 sts of cast-on edge, leaving center 12 sts of cast-on edge open. Sew band onto cast-on edge. Sew sleeve seams.

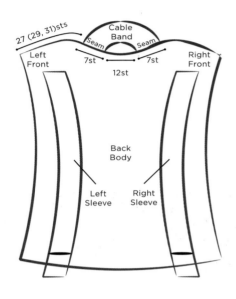

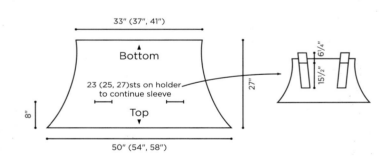

CABLE BAND PATTERN

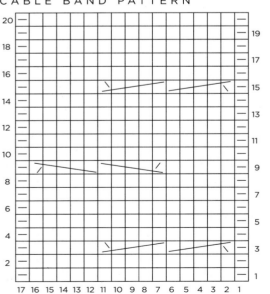

☐ = P on RS, K on WS

☐ = K on RS, P on WS

= C10L

= C10R

balthazar vest

SIZES XS (S, M, L)

KNITTED MEASUREMENTS
Bust: 25½" (28", 30½", 33") [65 (71, 77, 84)cm]
Back Length: 25¾" (26½", 27¼", 27¾") [65 (67, 69, 70.5)cm]

MATERIALS
605g (220 yds; 200m) of Twinkle Handknits Soft Chunky (100% merino wool; 83 yd/77 m per 200 g skein) in Sea or any super bulky weight yarn in the color of your choice

US size 17 (12.75mm) and 19 (15mm) 24" (61cm) circular needles

Stitch markers

GAUGE
9½ sts and 14½ rows = 6" (15cm) in St st on size 19 needles.

NOTES
Body is knit in one piece to neck shaping. Maintain Side Detail pattern until neck decreases consume stitches.

SPECIAL STITCHES
K2tog: Knit 2 together
SSK: Slip, slip, knit. Slip, slip, knit 2 together
yo: Yarn over

RIGHT SIDE DETAIL
RND 1 (RIGHT SIDE): K2tog, yo.

RND 2: Knit.

LEFT SIDE DETAIL
RND 1 (RIGHT SIDE): Yo, ssk.

RND 2: Knit.

RIGHT SIDE DETAIL

LEFT SIDE DETAIL

/ = K2tog
O = yo
— = P on RS, K on WS
\ = SSK

BODY
With smaller needles, CO 40 (44, 48, 52) sts. Pm to indicate beg of rnd. Join, being careful not to twist stitches. Rnd 1: *K1, p1; rep from *. Repeat this rnd until piece measures 5¾" (14.5cm).

Change to larger needles.

RND 1: K4 (5, 5, 6), work Right Side Detail over next 2 sts, k4 (4, 5, 5), pm, k20 (22, 24, 26) Back sts, pm, k4 (4, 5, 5), work Left Side Detail over next 2 sts, k4 (5, 5, 6).

Work two rnds even.

DIVIDE FOR NECK
Work even to end of round, slip marker, turn.

ROW 1 (WS): Purl.

ROW 2: Knit.

ROW 3: Purl.

ROW 4 (DEC ROW): K1, ssk, work to last 3 sts, k2tog, k1.

Dec 1 st each Neck edge every 8th row 3 more times. AT THE SAME TIME, when Body measures 15¾" (16", 16", 16") [40 (40.5, 40.5, 40.5)cm], and three Neck decreases have been worked, divide Body as follows:

RIGHT FRONT
K6 (7, 8, 9) Right Front sts, turn. Purl 1 row.

Next row (Armhole Dec): Work to last 3 sts, k2tog, k1. Cont on Right Front sts only, complete Neck shaping and work even until Right Front measures 24¾" (25", 25⅞", 26⅝") [63 (63.5, 66, 67.5)cm] from beg. BO remaining 4 (5, 6, 7) sts.

BACK

With RS facing, BO 2 sts, knit 18 (20, 22, 24) Back sts, turn. Purl 1 row.

Work even until Back measures 23½" (24¼", 25", 25½") [60 (61.5, 63.5, 65)cm] from beg.

BACK SHOULDER SHAPING

BO 1 st each Back Armhole Edge 4 (5, 6, 6) times. BO remaining 10 (10, 10, 12) sts.

LEFT FRONT

With RS facing, BO 2 sts, knit remaining 6 (7, 8, 10) Left Front sts. Purl 1 row.

Next row (Armhole Dec): K1, ssk, knit to end.

Complete Neck shaping and work even until Left Front measures same as Right Front. BO remaining 4 (5, 6, 7) sts.

SLEEVE CAP

Sew Front Shoulders to Back Shoulders.

With RS facing, with smaller needles, pick up 23 (23, 25, 27) sts around one Armhole.

SHORT-ROW SHAPING

Note: See page 78 for tips on wrapping and turning short-row shaping Row 1 (WS): K1, *p1, k1; rep from *. Pattern across 20 (20, 22, 24) sts, wrap and turn. Pattern across 17 (17, 19, 21) sts, wrap and turn. Pattern across 14 (14, 16, 18) sts, wrap and turn. Pattern across 11 (11, 13, 15) sts, wrap and turn. Pattern across 8 (8, 10, 12) sts, wrap and turn. Pattern across 5 (5, 7, 9) sts, wrap and turn.

BO all sts. Repeat for second Armhole.

NECKBAND

With RS facing, with smaller needles, pick up and knit 32 (33, 34, 35) sts up Right Front Neck edge, 10 (10, 10 12) sts across Back Neck, and 32 (33, 34, 35) sts down Left Front Neck edge—74 (76, 78, 82) sts. Row 1: *K1, p1; rep from *. Work 5 more rows in k2, p2 rib as established. Bind off. Weave in ends.

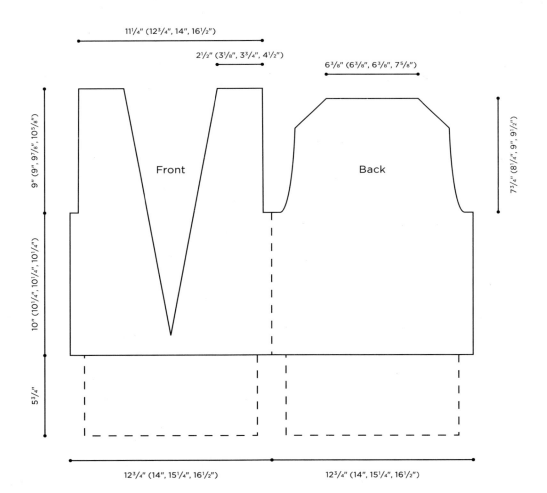

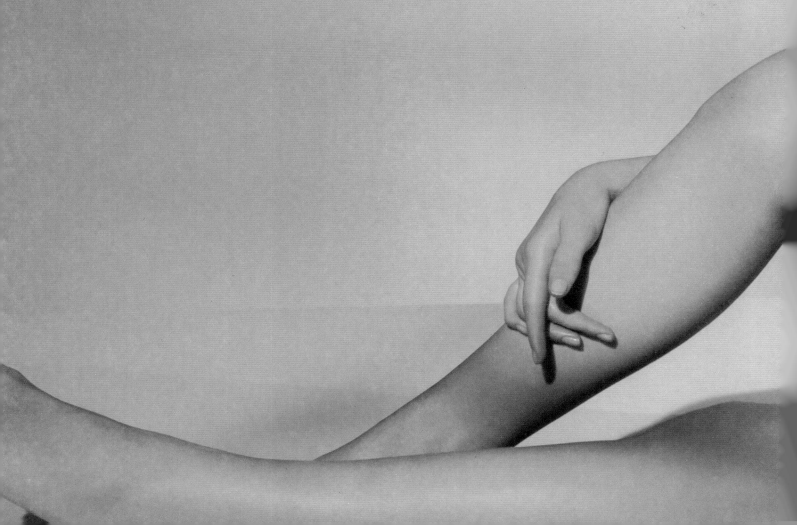

resort

sexy seaside sweater

WAVE PATTERN

RNDS 1–2 (RS): Knit.

RND 3: ★(K2tog) twice, (yo, k1) 4 times, (k2tog) twice; rep from ★.

RND 4: Purl.

Rep Rnds 1–4.

WAVE PATTERN

☐ = K on RS, P on WS	
╱ = K2tog	
◯ = yo	
⊟ = P on RS	

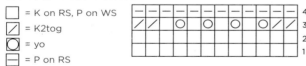

SLEEVES

(MAKE 2)

With medium needles, CO 23 (23, 25, 25) sts. Work 10 (8, 8, 8) rows even in St st, begin with a knit row. Next Row (Inc Row): K1, m1, knit to last 2 sts, m1, k1. Rep Inc Row every 6th row 0 (0, 0, 2) times and every 10th (8th, 8th, 8th) row 2 (3, 3, 2) times—29 (31, 33, 35) sts. Work even 9 (7, 7, 3) rows.

CAP SHAPING

BO 1 st at beg of next 16 (18, 20, 22) rows. BO rem 13 sts.

SIZES XS (S, M, L)

KNITTED MEASUREMENTS
Bust: 27" (28½", 30", 31½") [68.5 (72, 76, 80)cm]
Length: 18¾" (19½", 20", 20¾") [48 (49.5, 51, 53)cm]

MATERIALS
11 (12, 14) skeins of Twinkle Handknits Cruise (70% silk, 30% cotton; 120 yd/112 m per 50 g skein) in Mint (A); 1 skein in Periwinkle (B); 1 skein in Black (C); 1 skein in Tea Rose (D) *or* 1220 yd/112 m of any DK weight yarn in (B) color or the color of your choice; 89 yd/82m of any DK weight yarn in (C) color or the color of your choice; 72 yd/66m of any DK weight yarn in (D) color or the color of your choice

US size 13 (9mm), 15 (10mm), and 17 (12.75mm) 24" circular needles

Size L/11(8mm) crochet hook

Stitch holders

Stitch markers

GAUGE
Holding 4 strands together, 10 sts and 12½ rows = 4" (10 cm) in St st on size 15 needles

NOTE
This sweater is worked in the round to the shoulders. Yarn is held with 4 strands together throughout.

SPECIAL STITCHES
ch: Chain stitch
k2tog: Knit 2 together
sc: Single crochet
sl st: Slip stitch (crochet)
yo: Yarn over

BODY

With A and the largest needles, loosely cast on 84 (96, 108, 120) sts. Pm to indicate beg of rnd. Join, being careful not to twist sts.

Work Wave Pattern for 20 rows.

Dec Rnd: With B and the smallest needles, begin k1, p1 rib, decreasing 20 (28, 36, 44) sts evenly spaced—64 (68, 72, 76) sts. Place a second marker between stitches 32 and 33 (34 and 35, 36 and 37, 38 and 39) to indicate Underarm.

Cont in k1, p1 rib, work a total of 4 rnds each B, A, and D.

Front diagram measurements:
- 12³⁄₄" (13¹⁄₂", 14¹⁄₄", 15")
- 8"
- 9¹⁄₂" (10¹⁄₈", 10³⁄₄", 11³⁄₈")
- 5"
- 7¹⁄₂"
- 6¹⁄₄" (7", 7¹⁄₂", 8¹⁄₄")
- 20" (22³⁄₄", 25¹⁄₂", 28¹⁄₂")
- 10" (10¹⁄₂", 11", 11¹⁄₂")
- 13¹⁄₂" (14¹⁄₄", 15", 15³⁄₄")

Front

Back

BODICE SHAPING

Slip first 32 (34, 36, 38) Back sts onto holder. Join D at left Underarm marker. Working back and forth in k1, p1 rib on front sts only, with D and smaller needles, BO 5 sts at beg of next 6 (4, 2, 0) rows and 6 sts at beg of next 0 (2, 4, 6) rows. BO rem 2 sts.

Join A at Center Front. Pick up and knit 16 (17, 18, 19) sts from bound-off edge, pm to indicate right Underarm; on Back sts, k1, m1, k 30 (32, 34, 36), m1, k1, pm to indicate left Underarm; pick up and knit 16 (17, 18, 19) sts from bound-off sts—66 (70, 74, 78) sts.

Working back and forth, work even in St st for 5 more rows.

Next row: On Left Front sts, purl, on Back sts, p1, m1, p32 (34, 36, 38), m1, p1, on Right Front sts, purl—68 (72, 76, 80) sts.

Note: Read through all neck and body shaping before continuing.

Next Row: K1, ssk, knit to last 3 sts of rnd, k2tog, k1—66 (70, 74, 78) sts. Work 2 rows even in St st.

SHAPE RIGHT FRONT NECK AND DIVIDE FOR ARMHOLES

K1, ssk, k10 (11, 12, 13) Right Front sts, BO 2 sts, k34 (36, 38, 40) Back sts. Place rem 15 (16, 17, 18) sts on holder for Underarm and Left Front, turn.

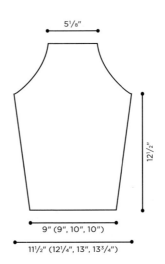

Sleeve diagram measurements:
- 5¹⁄₈"
- 12¹⁄₂"
- 9" (9", 10", 10")
- 11¹⁄₂" (12¹⁄₄", 13", 13³⁄₄")

Working on Back sts only, work 1 row even. BO 1 st at beg of next 2 rows. Work even for 16 (18, 20, 22) more rows.

SHOULDER AND NECK SHAPING

K6 (7, 8, 9) sts and place on holder for Right Shoulder, BO next 20 Back Neck sts, k6 (7, 8, 9) sts and place on holder for Left Shoulder.

With RS facing, rejoin A at left Underarm. BO 2 sts, work to last 3 sts, k2tog, k1.

Working on Left Front sts only, work 1 row even. BO 1 st at beg of next row. Cont to decrease 1 st at Neck edge every 3rd row 5 more times, making WS decreases as follows: P1, ssp, purl to end. [6 (7, 8, 9) sts remain when shaping is complete.] Work even 2 rows.

With WS facing, rejoin A at right Underarm. BO 1 st, purl to end.

Cont to decrease 1 st at Neck edge every 3rd row 5 more times, making WS decreases as follows: Purl to last 3 sts, ssp, p1. [6 (7, 8, 9) sts remain when shaping is complete.] Work even 2 rows.

FINISHING
Join Left and Right Shoulders with 3-needle bind-off.

With RS facing and using D, join yarn at Right Shoulder seam. Ch-1, sc 67 (70, 73, 79) sts evenly around, join with sl st to beg ch.

PICOT BORDER
Ch 1, *sc in next 3 sc, ch 3, sl st in 3rd ch from hook; rep from *. Fasten off. Weave in ends.

PICOT CROCHET BORDER

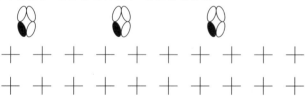

1 Repeat

+ = SC
○ = CH
● = sl st (crochet)

coco jacket

SIZES S (M, L)

KNITTED MEASUREMENTS
Bust: 30" (31¾", 33¼") [76 (80.5, 84.5)cm]
Length: 22¾" (23¼", 23¾") [58 (59, 60)cm]

MATERIALS
15 (17, 20) skeins of Twinkle Handknits Cruise (70% silk, 30% cotton; 120 yd/112 m per 50 g ball) in Dew (A); 1 skein in Sun Flower (B) *or* 1,319 yd/1,202 m of any DK weight yarn in the color of your choice

US size 15 (10mm) 24" (61cm) circular needles, or size needed to get gauge

Size L/11 (8mm) crochet hook

Stitch markers

Stitch holders

Five 1½" (4cm) buttons

GAUGE
Knitting 4 strands together, 10 sts and 12½ rows = 4" (10cm) in St st on size 15 needles

NOTES
This sweater is worked with 4 strands held together throughout. It is knit back and forth on a circular needle. Body is worked in one piece to the underarm. Make all pockets first.

SPECIAL STITCHES
ch: Chain stitch
dc: Double crochet
sc: Single crochet

SHELL EDGING
(MULT OF 3 + 1)

ROW 1: Ch–1, turn, sc into each dc across.

ROW 2: Ch–1, turn, *ch–3, 2 dc into same st, sk 2 sc, sc into next sc; rep from *.

CROCHET SHELL EDGING

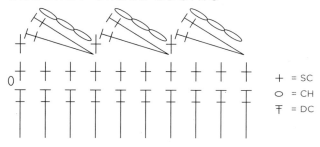

0

+ = SC
o = CH
Ŧ = DC

UPPER POCKETS
(MAKE 2)
With A, CO 10 sts. Beg St st and work 12 rows.

Place sts on holder.

BODY
With A, CO 74 (78, 82) sts.

ROW 1 (RS): K18 (19, 20), pm, k38 (40, 42) pm, k18 (19, 20).

Work even in St st for 3 (3, 5) more rows. Next row (Dec Row): *Knit to 3 sts before marker, k2tog, k1, sl marker, k1, ssk; rep from * once, knit to end—70 (74, 78) sts. Work even 5 (5, 3) rows.

JOIN LOWER POCKETS
K4, place next 10 sts on holder and hold at front of work, k10 sts from one Lower Pocket holder, k42 (46, 50), place next 10 sts on

LOWER POCKETS
(MAKE 2)
With A, CO 10 sts. Beg st st and work 10 rows. Place sts on holder.

holder and hold at front of work, k10 sts from remaining Lower Pocket holder, k4. Work even 1 (1, 3) rows. Rep Dec Row—66 (70, 74) sts. Work even 7 rows. Next Row (Inc Row): Knit to 1 st before marker, m1, k1, sl marker, k1, m1; rep from ★ once, knit to end. Rep Inc Row every 8th row once more—74 (78, 82) sts. Work even until Body measures 11½" (11¾", 12") [29 (30, 30.5)cm], ending with a WS row.

DIVIDE BODY AND JOIN POCKET

K4, place next 10 Pocket sts on holder and hold at front of work, k10 sts from one Upper Pocket holder, k3 (4, 5) sts, place 17 (18, 19) sts just knit onto a holder, BO 2, k36 (38, 40) Back sts, place remaining Left Front sts on holder.

BACK

Beg on WS, bind off 1 st at beg of next two rows. Work even 14 (15, 16) rows.

SHAPE SHOULDERS

BO 2 sts at beg of next 8 rows. BO rem 18 (20, 22) sts.

LEFT FRONT

Place Left Front sts on needle.

SHAPE ARMHOLE AND JOIN POCKET

With RS facing, BO 2 sts at beg of row, k3 (4, 5), place next 10 Pocket sts on holder and hold at front of work, k10 sts from remaining Upper Pocket holder, k4.

Cont in St st, bind off 1 st at Armhole edge once—16 (17, 18) sts. Work even until Left Front measures 17" (17¼", 17½") [43 (44, 44.5)cm], ending with a RS row.

NECK SHAPING

BO 3 sts at neck edge once, 2 sts once, and 1 st 3 times. BO rem 8 (9, 10) sts.

RIGHT FRONT

Place Right Front sts on needle. Beg on WS, bind off 1 st at Armhole once. Work even until Right Front measures same as Left Front to Neck shaping, ending with a WS row. At Neck edge, BO 3 sts once, 2 sts once, and 1 st 3 times. BO rem 8 (9, 10) sts.

SLEEVE
(MAKE 2)

With A, cast on 19 sts. Work 4 rows in St st. Inc 1 st each side next and every 10 (8, 7) rows 4 (5, 6) times—29 (31, 33) sts. Work even until Sleeve measures 17" (43cm).

CAP SHAPING

BO 1 st at beg of next 18 (20, 22) rows. BO rem 11 sts.

FINISHING

Sew Front Shoulders to sloped portion of Back Shoulders.

SLEEVE EDGING

With RS facing and crochet hook, join B at lower edge of Sleeve. Ch-3, dc into each cast-on st—19 dc. Work Shell Edging. Fasten off. Set in Sleeves and sew Sleeve seams.

LOWER EDGING

With RS facing, join B at lower Left Front edge. Ch-3, dc 74 (78, 82) sts across Bottom edge to Center Front. Work Shell Edging. Fasten off.

BUTTONHOLE BAND

Place markers on Right Front edge for 5 buttonholes, the first in the center of the Lower Edging and the last ½" (1cm) below Neck edge and 3 evenly spaced between. With RS facing and crochet hook, join B. Ch-3 (counts as dc), dc 42 (42, 45) sts up Right Front edge. Next row (buttonhole row) Ch-1, ★sc to buttonhole mark, ch-1, sk 1 sc; rep from ★ rep from ★ 4 times, sc to end of row. Work Row 2 of Shell Edging. Fasten off.

BUTTON BAND

On Left Front edge, work as for Buttonhole Band, omitting buttonholes. Fasten off.

NECK EDGING

With RS facing, join B at top edge of Buttonhole Band, ch-3 (counts as dc), dc 26 (30, 33) sts around Neck edge to end of Buttonhole Band. Work Shell Edging around Neck. Fasten off. Weave in ends.

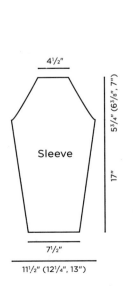

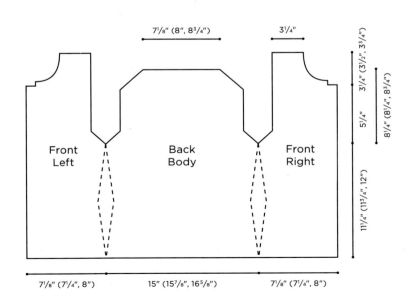

st. bart's mini

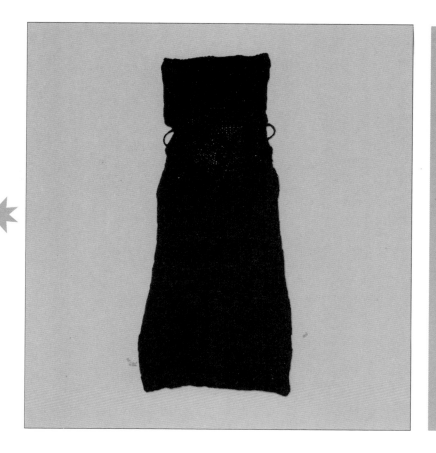

SIZES S (M, L)

KNITTED MEASUREMENTS
Bust: 28½" (30", 31½") [72 (76, 80)cm]
Front Length (excluding funnel neck):
31¼"(32", 32¾") [79 (81, 83)cm]

MATERIALS
14 (16, 18) skeins of Twinkle Handknits
Cruise (70% silk, 30% cotton; 120 yd/112 m
per 50 g skein) in Black *or* 1,628 yd/1,484
m of any DK weight yarn in the color of
your choice

US size 13 (9mm) and size 15 (10mm) 24"
(61cm) circular needles

Size L/11 (8mm) crochet hook

Stitch markers

Stitch holders

GAUGE
Knitting 4 strands together, 10 sts and 12½
rows = 4" (10cm) in St st on size 15
needles

NOTES
Knit holding 4 strands together throughout.
Body is knit in the round.

BODY

With smaller needles, CO 88 (92, 96) sts.
Pm to indicate beg of rnd. Join, being careful not to twist stitches. Rnd 1: *K1, p1;
rep from *. Work 11 more rnds k1, p1 rib
as established. Change to larger needles and
St st.

K44 (46, 48), pm, k44 (46, 48). Work even
until piece measures 11" (28cm) from beg.

Next Rnd (Dec Rnd): *K9, ssk, k to 11
sts before marker, k2tog, k9; rep from * 1
time—84 (88, 92) sts.

Work Dec Rnd every 6th rnd 4 more
times—68 (72, 76) sts.

Work even 10 rnds.

SHAPE BODY AND BEGIN
BOBBLES (SEE PAGE 75)
K1, m1, knit to 1 st before marker, m1,
k1, sl marker, k1, m1, k15 (16, 17), make
bobble (see page 76), k16 (17, 18), m1,
k1—72 (76, 80) sts.

Work even 3 rnds.

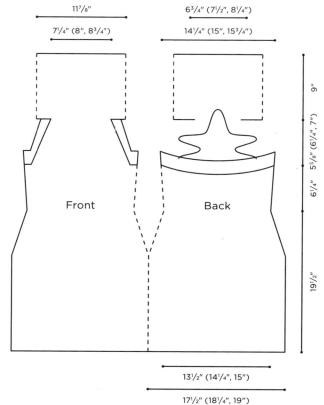

11⁷⁄₈"

6¾" (7½", 8¼")

7¼" (8", 8¾")

14¼" (15", 15¾")

9"

5⁵⁄₈" (6¼", 7")

6¼"

Front

Back

19½"

13½" (14¼", 15")

17½" (18¼", 19")

Second bobble round: Knit across Back sts, k18 (19, 20), make bobble (see page 76), MB, k17 (18, 19).

Alternating bobble sts every 4 rnds, work even until piece measures 24" (61cm) from beg.

DIVIDE BODY

Knit 39 (41, 43) Back and Underarm sts and place on holder, k15 (16, 17) Front sts, pm, k15 (16, 17) Front sts, place remaining 3 Underarm sts on holder, turn.

Continuing bobbles until 7 bobbles are complete, shape Front as follows:

Work even 1 (WS) row. BO 1 st at beg of next 8 rows. Work 2 rows even BO 1 st at beg of next 4 rows—18 (20, 22) sts rem.

Work even 2 rows. Place Front sts on holder.

BAND (ARMHOLE THROUGH BACK)

With smaller needles and RS facing, pick up 59 (63, 67) sts around Left Front Neck edge, Underarms, Back and Right Front Neck edge. Row 1 (WS): P1, *k1, p1; rep from *. Work 4 more rows in k1, p1 rib as established. BO loosely.

COLLAR

With larger needles, knit Front sts, pick up 4 sts and knit 4 sts from edge of ribbing, CO 34 (32, 30) sts, pick up and knit 4 sts from edge of ribbing, pm—60 sts. Work 28 rnds of St st (knit every rnd). BO loosely.

FINISHING

With crochet hook, crochet two chains each 10" (10½", 11") [25 (26.5, 28)cm] long. Sew one end to each corner of Front Neck. Sew other ends to Back ribbing, tering 17 (19, 21) sts between straps.

hamptons halter

SIZES XS (S, M, L)

KNITTED MEASUREMENTS
Bust: 25" (26½", 28", 29½") [63.5 (67, 71, 75)cm]
Length: 23⅛", (24¼", 25⅜", 26⅜") [59 (61.5, 64.5, 67)cm]

MATERIALS
9 (10, 12) skeins of Twinkle Handknits Cruise (70% silk, 30% cotton; 120 yd/112 m per 50 g skein) in Periwinkle *or* 1,018 yd/928 m of any DK weight yarn in the color of your choice

US size 13 (9mm) and 15 (10mm) 24" (61cm) circular knitting needles

Size L/11 (8mm) crochet hook

Stitch holders

Stitch markers

GAUGE
Holding 4 strands together, 12 sts and 12 rows = 4" (10cm) in k1, p1 rib, relaxed, on size 13 needles

NOTES
This sweater is worked in the round. Yarn is held with 4 strands together throughout.

SPECIAL STITCHES
k2tog: Knit 2 together
m1: make 1
S2KP: Slip 2 sts together as if to k, k1, p2sso (pass 2 sl sts over)
SSK: Slip, slip, knit 2 together
yo: Yarn over

RIGHT FRONT   LEFT FRONT

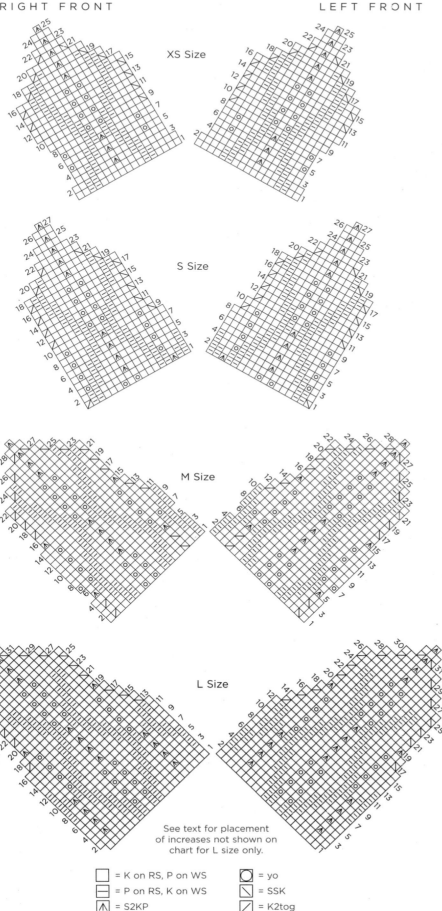

XS Size

S Size

M Size

L Size

See text for placement
of increases not shown on
chart for L size only.

□ = K on RS, P on WS   ○ = yo

⊟ = P on RS, K on WS   ◿ = SSK

◣ = S2KP   ◤ = K2tog

LACY LEAF PATTERN
(MULT OF 14 STS)

RND 1: *P2, k9, p2, k1; rep from *.

RND 2: *Yo, p2, k3, s2kp, k3, p2, yo, k1; rep from *.

RND 3: *K1, p2, k7, p2, k2; rep from *.

RND 4: *Yo, k1, p2, k2, s2kp, k2, p2, k1, yo, k1; rep from *.

RND 5: *K2, p2, k5, p2, k3; rep from *.

RND 6: *Yo, k2, p2, k1, s2kp, k1, p2, k2, yo, k1; rep from *.

RND 7: *K3, p2, k3, p2, k4; rep from *.

RND 8: *Yo, k3, p2, s2kp, p2, k3, yo, k1; rep from *.

RND 9: *K4, p2, k1, p2, k5; rep from *—
15 sts.

RND 10: *K1, *K3, p2, yo, k1, yo, p2, k3, s2kp; rep from *. (Move end-of-round marker on last repeat.)

RND 11: *(K3, p2) twice, k4; rep from *.

RND 12: K1, * K2, p2, (k1, yo) twice, k1, p2, k2, s2kp; rep from *. (Move end-of-round marker on last repeat.)

RND 13: K1, *K2, p2, k5, p2, k3; rep from *.

RND 14: K1, *k1, p2, k2 (yo, k1) twice, k1, p2, k1, s2kp; rep from *. (Move end-of-round marker on last repeat.)

RND 15: *K1, p2, k7, p2, k2; rep from *.

RND 16: K1, *P2, k3, (yo, k1) twice, k2, p2, s2kp; rep from *. (move end of round marker on last repeat.)

Rep Rnds 1–16.

RIGHT FRONT PATTERN
SIZE XS ONLY

ROW 1 (RS): K4, p2, k7, p2, k2—17 sts.

ROW 2: P2, k2, p7, k2, p4.

ROW 3: K4, p2, k2, s2kp, k2, p2, k2—15 sts.

ROW 4: P2, k2, p5, k2, p4.

ROW 5: K2, yo, k2, p2, k1, s2kp, k1, p2, k2, yo.

LACY LEAF PATTERN

∧	—	—			○		○				—	—		16
		—	—								—	—		15
∧		—	—		○		○				—	—		14
		—	—						—	—				13
∧		—	—		○		○		—	—				12
			—	—				—	—					11
∧			—	—	○		○	—	—					10
			—	—			—	—						9
	○			—	—	∧	—	—			○			8
			—	—		∧		—	—					7
	○			—		∧		—	—		○			6
			—	—		∧		—	—					5
	○			—	—	∧	—	—			○			4
		—	—					—	—					3
	○	—	—			∧		—	—	○				2
	—	—					—	—						1

- ─ = P on RS, K on WS
- ☐ = K on RS, P on WS
- ○ = yo
- ∧ = S2KP

ROW 6: (P3, k2) twice, p5.

ROW 7: K2, yo, k3, p2, s2kp, p2, k3, yo.

ROW 8: P4, k2, p1, k2, p6.

ROW 9: Ssk, k4, p2, yo, k1, yo, p2, k4—16 sts.

ROW 10: P4, k2, p3, k2, p5.

ROW 11: Ssk, k3, p2, (k1, yo) twice, k1, p2, k4—17 sts.

ROW 12: P4, k2, p5, k2, p4.

ROW 13: Ssk, k2, p2, k2, yo, k1, yo, k2, p2, k2, k2tog.

ROW 14: P3, k2, p7, k2, p3.

ROW 15: Ssk, k1, p2, k3, yo, k1, yo, k3, p2, k1, k2tog.

ROW 16: P2, k2, p9, k2, p2.

ROW 17: Ssk, p2, k3, s2kp, k3, p2, k2tog—13 sts.

ROW 18: P1, k2, p7, k2, p1.

ROW 19: Ssk, p1, k2, s2kp, k1, p1, k2tog—9 sts.

ROW 20: K2, p5, k2.

ROW 21: SSK, k1, s2kp, k1, k2tog—5 sts.

ROW 22: Purl.

ROW 23: K1, s2kp, k1—3 sts.

ROW 24: Purl.

ROW 25: S2kp.

Do not fasten off.

SIZE S ONLY

ROW 1 (RS): P2, s2kp, p2, k3, yo, k1, yo, k3, p2, k2tog—17 sts.

ROW 2: P1, k2, p9, k2, p1, k2.

ROW 3: P1, k2, yo, p2, k3, s2kp, k3, p2, yo, k1.

ROW 4: P2, k2, p7, k2, p3, k1.

ROW 5: K3, yo, k1, p2, k2, s2kp, k2, p2, k1, yo, k1.

ROW 6: P3, (k2, p5) twice.

ROW 7: K3, yo, k2, p2, k1, s2kp, k1, p2, k2, yo, k1.

ROW 8: P4, k2, p3, k2, p6.

ROW 9: Ssk, k1, yo, k3, p2, s2kp, p2, k3, yo, k1—16 sts.

ROW 10: P5, k2, p1, k2, p6.

ROW 11: Ssk, k3, p2, yo, k1, yo, p2, k3, k2tog—15 sts.

ROW 12: P4, k2, p3, k2, p4.

ROW 13: Ssk, k2, p2, (k1, yo) twice, k1, p2, k2, k2tog—14 sts.

ROW 14: P3, k2, p5, k2, p3.

ROW 15: Ssk, k1, p2, k2, yo, k1, yo, k2, p2, k1, k2tog.

ROW 16: P2, k2, p7, k2, p2.

ROW 17: Ssk, p2, k3, yo, k1, yo, k3, p2, k2tog—15 sts.

ROW 18: P1, k2, p9, k2, p1.

ROW 19: Ssk, p1, k3, s2kp, k3, p1, k2tog—11 sts.

ROW 20: P1, k1, p7, k1, p1.

ROW 21: Ssk, k2, s2kp, k2, k2tog—7 sts.

ROW 22: Purl.

ROW 23: K2, S2kp, k2—5 sts.

ROW 24: Purl.

ROW 25: K1, s2kp, k1.

ROW 26: Purl.

ROW 27: S2kp.

Do not fasten off.

SIZE M ONLY

ROW 1 (RS): P1, k2, ssk, k2, p2, (k1, yo) twice, k1, p2, k2, k2tog, k1—19 sts.

ROW 2: P4, (k2, p5) twice, k1.

ROW 3: P2, k1, ssk, k1, p2, k2, yo, k1, yo, k2, p2, k1, k2tog, k1.

ROW 4: P3, k2, p7, k2, p3, k2.

ROW 5: P2, s2kp, p2, k3, yo, k1, yo, k3, p2, s2kp—17 sts.

ROW 6: P1, k2, p9, k2, p1, k2.

ROW 7: P2, yo, k1, yo, p2, k3, s2kp, k3, p2, yo, k1, yo—19 sts.

ROW 8: P3, k2, p7, k2, p3, k2.

ROW 9: P1, k3, yo, k1, p2, k2, s2kp, k2, p2, k1, yo, k2.

ROW 10: P4, k2, p5, k2, p5, k1.

ROW 11: Ssk, k2, yo, k2, p2, k1, s2kp, k1, p2, k2, yo, k2—18 sts.

ROW 12: P5, k2, p3, k2, p6.

ROW 13: K2tog, k1, yo, k3, p2, s2kp, p2, k3, yo, k2—17 sts.

ROW 14: P6, k2, p1, k2, p6.

ROW 15: S2kp, k3, p2, yo, k1, yo, p2, k3, s2kp—15 sts.

ROW 16: P4, k2, p3, k2, p4.

ROW 17: Ssk, k2, p2, (k1, yo) twice, k1, p2, k2, k2tog.

ROW 18: P3, k2, p5, k2, p3.

ROW 19: Ssk, k1, p2, k2, yo, k1, yo, k2, p2, k1, k2tog.

ROW 20: P2, k2, p7, k2, p2.

ROW 21: Ssk, p2, k3, yo, k1, yo, k3, p2, k2tog.

ROW 22: P1, k2, p9, k2, p1.

ROW 23: Ssk, p1, k3, s2kp, k3, p1, k2tog—11 sts.

ROW 24: P1, k1, p7, k1, p1.

ROW 25: Ssk, k2, s2kp, k2, k2tog—7 sts.

ROW 26: Purl.

ROW 27: Ssk, s2kp, k2tog—3 sts.

ROW 28: Purl.

ROW 29: S2kp.

Do not fasten off.

SIZE L ONLY
ROW 1 (RS): K9, p2, k1, p2, k6—20 sts

ROW 2: P1, m1, p5, k1, p1, k2, p9—21 sts.

ROW 3: P1, m1, k2, s2kp, k3, p2, yo, k1, yo, p2, k3, s2kp, k1, m1.

ROW 4: P6, k2, p3, k2, p7, k1.

ROW 5: P1, m1, k2, s2kp, k2, p2, (k1, yo) twice, k1, p2, k2, s2kp, k1, m1.

ROW 6: (P5, k2) three times.

ROW 7: K1, m1, p1, k1, s2kp, k1, p2, k2, yo, k1, yo, k2, p2, k1, s2kp, k1, m1.

ROW 8: K1, p3, k2, p7, k2, p3, k2, p1.

ROW 9: K1, m1, p2, s2kp, p2, k3, yo, k1, yo, k3, p2, s2kp, ml, k1.

ROW 10: K2, p1, k2, p9, k2, p1, k2, p2.

ROW 11: K1, p2, k2, yo, p2, k3, s2kp, k3, p2, yo, k2, p1.

ROW 12: K1, p3, k2, p7, k2, p3, k2, p1.

ROW 13: Ssk, k3, yo, k1, p2, k2, s2kp, k2, p2, k1, yo, k3—20 sts.

ROW 14: (P5, k2) twice, p5, k1.

ROW 15: Ssk, k2, yo, k2, p2, k1, s2kp, k1, p2, k2, yo, k3—19 sts.

ROW 16: P6, k2, p3, k2, p6.

ROW 17: Ssk, k1, yo, k3, p2, s2kp, p2, k3, yo, k1, k2tog—17 sts.

ROW 18: P6, k2, p1, k2, p6.

ROW 19: S2kp, k3, p2, yo, k1, yo, p2, k3, s2kp—15 sts.

ROW 20: P4, k2, p3, k2, p4.

ROW 21: Ssk, k2, p2, (k1, yo) twice, k1, p2, k2, k2tog.

ROW 22: P3, k2, p5, k2, p3.

ROW 23: Ssk, k1, p2, k2, yo, k1, yo, k2, p2, k1, k2tog.

ROW 24: P2, k2, p7, k2, p2.

ROW 25: Ssk, p2, k3, yo, k1, yo, k3, p2, k2tog.

ROW 26: P1, k2, p9, k2, p1.

ROW 27: Ssk, p1, k3, s2kp, k3, p1, k2tog—11 sts.

ROW 28: P1, k1, p7, k1, p1.

ROW 29: Ssk, k2, s2kp, k2, k2tog—7 sts.

ROW 30: Purl.

ROW 31: Ssk, k2tog, s2kp.

ROW 32: Purl.

ROW 31: S2kp.

Do not fasten off.

**LEFT FRONT PATTERN
SIZE XS ONLY**
ROW 1 (RS): K2, p2, k7, p2, k4—17 sts.

ROW 2: P4, k2, p7, k2, p2.

ROW 3: K2, p2, k2, s2kp, k2, p2, k4—15 sts.

ROW 4: P4, k2, p5, k2, p2.

ROW 5: Yo, k2, p2, k1, s2kp, k1, p2, k2, yo, k2.

ROW 6: P5, (k2, p3) twice.

ROW 7: Yo, k3, p2, s2kp, p2, k3, yo, k2.

ROW 8: P6, k2, p1, k2, p4.

ROW 9: K4, p2, yo, k1, yo, p2, k4, k2tog—16 sts.

ROW 10: P5, k2, p3, k2, p4.

ROW 11: K4, p2, (k1, yo) twice, k1, p2, k3, k2tog—17 sts.

ROW 12: P4, k2, p5, k2, p4.

ROW 13: Ssk, k2, p2, k2, yo, k1, yo, k2, p2, k2, ktog.

ROW 14: P3, k2, p7, k2, p3.

ROW 15: Ssk, k1, p2, k3, yo, k1, yo, k3, p2, k1, ktog.

ROW 16: P2, k2, p9, k2, p2.

ROW 17: Ssk, p2, k3, s2kp, k3, p2, k2tog—13 sts.

ROW 18: P1, k2, p7, k2, p1.

ROW 19: Ssk, p1, k2, s2kp, k2, p1, k2tog—9 sts.

ROW 20: P1, k1, p5, k1, p1.

ROW 21: Ssk, k1, s2kp, k1, k2tog—5 sts.

ROW 22: Purl.

ROW 23: K1, s2kp, k1—3 sts.

ROW 24: Purl.

ROW 25: S2kp.

Do not fasten off.

SIZE S ONLY
ROW 1 (RS): Ssk, p2, k3, yo, k1, yo, k3, p2, s2kp, p2—17 sts.

ROW 2: K2, p1, k2, p9, k2, p1.

ROW 3: K1, yo, p2, k3, s2kp, k3, p2, yo, k2, p1.

ROW 4: K1, p3, k2, p7, k2, p2.

ROW 5: K1, yo, k1, p2, k2, s2kp, k2, p2, k1, yo, k3.

ROW 6: (P5, k2) twice, p3.

ROW 7: K1, yo, k2, p2, k1, s2kp, k1, p2, k2, yo, k3.

ROW 8: P6, k2, p3, k2, p4.

ROW 9: K1, yo, k3, p2, s2kp, p2, k3, yo, k1, ssk—16 sts.

ROW 10: P6, k2, p1, k2, p5.

ROW 11: Ssk, k3, p2, yo, k1, yo, p2, k3, k2tog—15 sts.

ROW 12: P4, k2, p3, k2, p4.

ROW 13: Ssk, k2, p2, (k1, yo) twice, k1, p2, k2, k2tog—14 sts.

ROW 14: P3, k2, p5, k2, p3.

ROW 15: Ssk, k1, p2, k2, yo, k1, yo, k2, p2, k1, k2tog.

ROW 16: P2, k2, p7, k2, p2.

ROW 17: Ssk, p2, k3, yo, k1, yo, k3, p2, K2tog—15.

ROW 18: P1, k2, p9, k2, p1.

ROW 19: Ssk, p1, k3, s2kp, k3, p1, k2tog—11 sts.

ROW 20: P1, k1, p7, k1, p1.

ROW 21: Ssk, k2, s2kp, k2, k2tog—7 sts.

ROW 22: Purl.

ROW 23: K2, s2kp, k2—5 sts.

ROW 24: Purl.

ROW 25: K1, s2kp, k1.

ROW 26: Purl.

ROW 27: S2kp.

Do not fasten off.

ROW 1 (RS): K1, ssk, k2, p2, (k1, yo) twice, k1, p2, k2, k2tog, k2, p1—19 sts.

ROW 2: K1, (p5, k2) twice, p4.

ROW 3: K1, ssk, k1, p2, k2, yo, k1, yo, k2, p2, k1, k2tog, k1, p2.

ROW 4: K2, p3, k2, p7, k2, p3.

ROW 5: S2kp, p2, k3, yo, k1, yo, k3, p2, s2kp, p2—17 sts.

ROW 6: K2, p1, k2, p9, k2, p1.

ROW 7: Yo, k1, yo, p2, k3, s2kp, k3, p2, yo, k1, yo, p2—19 sts.

ROW 8: K2, p3, k2, p7, k2, p3.

ROW 9: K2, yo, k1, p2, k2, s2kp, k2, p2, k1, yo, k3, p1.

ROW 10: K1, p5, k2, p5, k2, p4.

ROW 11: K2, yo, k2, p2, k1, s2kp, k1, p2, k2, yo, k2, ssk—18 sts.

ROW 12: P6, k2, p3, k2, p5.

ROW 13: K2, yo, k3, p2, s2kp, p2, k3, yo, k1, ssk—17 sts.

ROW 14: P6, k2, p1, k2, p6.

ROW 15: S2kp, k3, p2, yo, k1, yo, p2, k3, s2kp—15 sts.

ROW 16: P4, k2, p3, k2, p4.

ROW 17: Ssk, k2, p2, (k1, yo) twice, k1, p2, k2, k2tog—15 sts.

ROW 18: P3, k2, p5, k2, p3.

ROW 19: Ssk, k1, p2, k2, yo, k1, yo, k2, p2, k1, k2tog.

ROW 20: P2, k2, p7, k2, p2.

ROW 21: Ssk, p2, k3, yo, k1, yo, k3, p2, k2tog.

ROW 22: P1, k2, p9, k2, p1.

ROW 23: Ssk, p1, k3, s2kp, k3, p1, k2tog—11 sts.

ROW 24: P1, k1, p7, k1, p1.

ROW 25: Ssk, k2, s2kp, k2, k2tog—7 sts.

ROW 26: Purl.

ROW 27: Ssk, s2kp, k2tog—3 sts.

ROW 28: Purl.

ROW 29: S2kp.

Do not fasten off.

ROW 1 (RS): K6, p2, k1, p2, k9—20 sts.

ROW 2: P9, k2, p1, k2, p5, m1, p1—21 sts.

ROW 3: M1, k1, s2kp, k3, p2, yo, k1, yo, p2, k3, s2kp, k2, m1, p1.

ROW 4: K1, p7, k2, p3, k2, p6.

ROW 5: M1, k1, s2kp, k2, p2, (k1, yo) twice, k1, p2, k2, s2kp, k2, m1, p1.

ROW 6: (K2, p5) three times.

ROW 7: M1, k1, s2kp, k1, p2, k2, yo, k1, yo, k2, p2, k1, s2kp, k1, p1, m1, k1.

ROW 8: P1, k2, p3, k2, p7, k2, p3, k1.

ROW 9: K1, m1, s2kp, p2, k3, yo, k1, yo, k3, p2, s2kp, p2, ml, k1.

ROW 10: P2, k2, p1, k2, p9, k2, p1, k2.

ROW 11: P1, k2, yo, p2, k3, s2kp, k3, p2, yo, k2, p2, k1.

ROW 12: P1, k2, p3, k2, p7, k2, p3, k1.

ROW 13: K3, yo, k1, p2, k2, s2kp, k2, p2, k1, yo, k3, k2tog—20 sts.

ROW 14: P6, (k2, p5) twice.

ROW 15: K3, yo, k2, p2, k1, s2kp, k1, p2, k2, yo, k2, k2tog—19 sts.

ROW 16: P6, k2, p3, k2, p6.

ROW 17: Ssk, k1, yo, k3, p2, s2kp, p2, k3, yo, k1, k2tog—17 sts.

ROW 18: P6, k2, p1, k2, p6.

ROW 19: S2kp, k3, p2, yo, k1, yo, p2, k3, s2kp—15 sts.

ROW 20: P4, k2, p3, k2, p4.

ROW 21: Ssk, k2, p2, (k1, yo) twice, k1, p2, k2, k2tog.

ROW 22: P3, k2, p5, k2, p3.

ROW 23: Ssk, k1, p2, k2, yo, k1, yo, k2, p2, k1, k2tog.

ROW 24: P2, k2, p7, k2, p2.

ROW 25: Ssk, p2, k3, yo, k1, yo, k3, p2, k2tog.

ROW 26: P1, k2, p9, k2, p1.

ROW 27: Ssk, p1, k3, s2kp, k3, p1, k2tog—11 sts.

ROW 28: P1, k1, p7, k1, p1.

ROW 29: Ssk, k2, s2kp, k2, ssk—7 sts.

ROW 30: Purl.

ROW 31: Ssk, s2kp, k2tog.

ROW 32: Purl.

ROW 31: S2kp.

Do not fasten off.

BODY

With larger needles, loosely CO 98 (98, 112, 112) sts. Pm and join, being careful not to twist sts.

Work Lacy Leaf Pattern for 40 rnds. Piece measures approx 13" (33cm).

Dec Rnd: With smaller needles, begin k1, p1 rib, decreasing 30 (26, 36, 32) sts evenly spaced— 68 (72, 76, 80) sts.

Work k1, p1 rib for 3" (7.6cm). Place a second marker at the halfway point of the rnd [between stitches 34 and 35 (36 and 37, 38 and 39, 40 and 41)].

FRONT BODICE SHAPING

Cont in k1, p1 rib, work to 5 (5, 6, 6) sts from marker, wrap and turn, work to 5 (5, 6, 6) st from marker, wrap and turn, work to 10 (10, 12, 12) sts from marker, wrap

and turn, work to 10 (10, 12, 12) sts from marker, wrap and turn, work to 15 (15, 18, 18) sts from marker, wrap and turn, work to 15 (15, 18, 18) sts from marker, wrap and turn.

Work 2 (3, 1, 2) sts. You should now be at the Center Front.

Work Row 1 of Right Front pattern over next 17 (18, 19, 20) sts, rib to last 17 (18, 19, 20) sts, work Left Front pattern to end. Turn.

Work one row even in established patterns.

NEXT ROW (INC ROWS): Work across Right Front sts, sl marker, inc 1, pattern to next marker, inc 1, sl marker, work across Left Front sts—70 (74, 78, 82) sts.

Work even 2 rows.

NEXT ROW (INC ROWS): Work across Left Front sts, sl marker, inc 1, pattern to next marker, inc 1, sl marker, work across Right Front sts—72 (76, 80, 84) sts. Work in established patterns 0 (2, 4, 6) more rows

RIGHT SIDE AND SHORT-ROW SHAPING
Note: Remember to work shaping at Center Front edges on the following rows.
Begin Right Front Pattern over Right Front sts, rib next 13 Back sts, wrap and turn.

Work 13 Back and all Right Front sts, turn.

Work Right Front sts, rib next 7 sts, wrap and turn.

Pattern across 7 Back and all Right Front sts, turn.

Work across Right Front sts, rib across Back sts, begin Left Front Pattern over Left Front sts.

LEFT SIDE AND SHORT-ROW SHAPING
NEXT ROW (WS): Work Left Front sts, rib next 13 Back sts, wrap and turn.

Work 13 Back sts and all Left Front sts.

Work Left Front sts, rib next 7 Back sts, wrap and turn.

Work 7 Back sts and all Left Front sts.

Work Left Front sts, place these sts on holder, BO 38 (40, 42, 44) Back sts, pattern across Right Front sts.

Working back and forth on Right Front sts, work until Row 25 (27, 29, 31) of pattern is complete. Sl last st onto crochet hook and chain 25" (63.5cm). Fasten off.

Place Left Front sts on needle. Working back and forth on Left Front sts only, work until Row 25 (27, 29, 31) of pattern is complete. Sl last st onto crochet hook and chain 25" (63.5cm). Fasten off. Weave in ends.

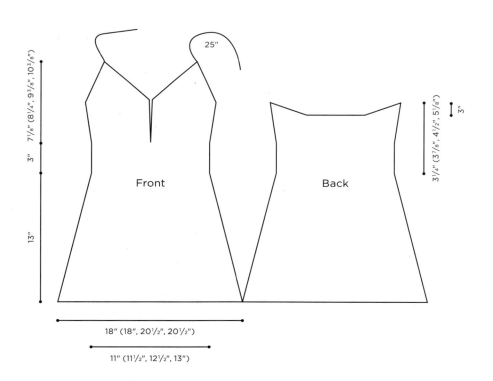

twiggy tunic

SIZES XS (S, M, L)

KNITTED MEASUREMENTS
Bust: 22" (23½", 25", 26½") [56 (60, 63.5, 67)cm]
Back Length (including neck rib band): 27⅛" (28¾", 29⅜", 30") [69 (73, 74.5, 76)cm]

MATERIALS
14 (16, 18) skeins of Twinkle Handknits Cruise (70% silk. 30% cotton; 120 yd/112 m per 50 g skein) in Mauve *or* 1,596/1,455 m of any DK weight yarn in the color of your choice

US size 15 (10mm) 24" (61cm) circular needles

Stitch holders

Cable needle

GAUGE
10 sts and 12½ rows = 4" (10cm) in reverse St st on size 15 (10mm) needles

NOTES
The sleeves are knit first, then the body. Sleeves are joined to the body at underarm and sweater is knit in one piece from that point on.

SPECIAL STITCHES
C4R (Cable 4 right): Slip next 2 sts to cable needle and hold in back of work, K2, K2 from cable needle
T2R (Twist 2 right): Knit next 2 sts together, leaving sts on left-hand needle, K first st again, slip both sts off needle
T2LP (Twist 2 left purl): Sl next st onto cable needle and hold in front, p1, k1 from cable needle
T2RP (Twist 2 right pull): Sl next st onto cable needle and hold in back, k1, p1 from cable needle.

TWIGGY CABLE

ROW 1 (RIGHT SIDE): Knit.

ROWS 2 AND 4: Purl.

ROW 3: C4R.

ROW 5: Knit.

ROW 6: Purl.

Repeat Rows 1–6.

TWIGGY SLEEVE STITCH PATTERN

☐ = K on RS, P on WS

⤬ = C4R

TWIGGY CENTER PANEL
(OVER 15 STS)

RND 1: P5, T2RP, k1, T2LP, p5.

RND 2: P5, (k1, p1) twice, k1, p5.

RND 3: P4, T2RP, p1, k1, p1, T2LP, p4.

RND 4: P4, k1, p2, k1, p2, k1, p4.

RND 5: P3, T2RP, p2, k1, p2, T2LP, p3.

RND 6: (P3, k1) 3 times, p3.

RND 7: P2, T2RP, p3, k1, p3, T2LP, p2.

RND 8: P2, k1, p4, k1, p4, k1, p2.

RND 9: P2, knit into the (front, back, front) of the next st, p4, k1, p4, knit into the

(Front, Back, Front) of the next st,
p2—19 sts.

RND 10: P2, (k3, p3) 2 times, k3, p2.

RND 11: P2, s2kp, p2, T2RP, k1, T2LP, p2, s2kp, p2.

Rep Rnds 2–11 6 (7, 7, 7) more times, working final rnd of
pattern as follows:

P2, s2kp, p4, k1, p4, s2kp, p2.

If additional rnds are needed for your size, continue pattern as:
P7, k1, p7.

TWIGGY CENTER PANEL

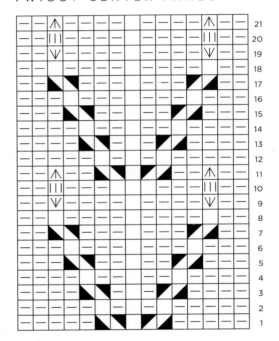

- ☐ = P on RS, K on WS
- ◤ = T2RP:
- ☐ = K on RS, P on WS
- ◥ = T2LP
- ⋀ = S2KP
- ||| = K3
- ⋁ = K into (front, bank, front) of next st

LEFT SLEEVE

CO 21 (23, 25, 27) sts. Row 1 (RS): K1, *p2, k2; rep from * to
last 2 sts, p 0 (2, 0, 2). Work 7 more rows in k2, p2 rib as established.

Next row (RS): P9 (10, 11, 12), work Twiggy Cable over next 4
sts, p8 (9, 10, 11). Cont in reverse St st each side of cable, work 7
more rows.

Next row (inc row): P1, m1, purl to last st, m1, p1—23 (25, 27, 29)
sts. Cont in established pattern, inc 1 st each side every 8th row 4
more times—31 (33, 35, 37) sts. Work even until piece measures
16" (40.5cm) from beg, ending with a WS row.

UNDERARM SHAPING
BO 3 sts at beg of next row and 2 sts at beg of following row.
Place rem 26 (28, 30, 32) sts on holder.

RIGHT SLEEVE

CO 21 (23, 25, 27) sts. Row 1 (RS): K1, *p2, k2; rep from *. Work
7 more rows in k2, p2 rib as established.

Next row (RS): P8 (9, 10, 11), work Twiggy Cable over next 4 sts,
p9 (10, 11, 12). Shape as for Left Sleeve until Sleeve measures
approximately 16" (40.5cm), ending with a WS row.

UNDERARM SHAPING
BO 2 sts at beg of next row and 3 sts at beg of foll row. Place rem
26 (28, 30, 32) sts on holder.

BODY

CO 56 (60, 64, 68) sts. Pm to indicate beg of rnd. Join, being careful not to twist stitches.

RND 1: *K2, p2; rep from *. Work 7 more rnds in k2, p2 rib as
established.

Next rnd: P3 (4, 5, 6), k4, p7, m1, p7, k4, p3 (4, 5, 6), pm to indicate Underarm, purl to end of round—57 (61, 65, 69) sts.

Next rnd (establish pattern): P3 (4, 5, 6), work Twiggy Cable over
next 4 sts, work Center Panel over next 15 sts, work Twiggy Cable
over next 4 sts, purl to end of rnd. Work even in established patterns until 60 rnds of Center Panel are complete, ending last rnd 2
sts before end of rnd.

UNDERARM SHAPING
BO 4 sts, pattern across next 25 (27, 29, 31) Front sts, BO 4 sts,
purl across Back sts to end of rnd, pm.

JOIN SLEEVES AND BODY
Maintaining established st patterns, work 26 (28, 30, 32) Left
Sleeve sts, pm, work Front sts, pm, work 26 (28, 30, 32) Right
Sleeve sts, pm, work Back sts—101 (109, 117, 125) sts. Work 1
round even.

RAGLAN SHAPING

Note: Read all instructions for raglan shaping before beginning.

Next rnd (dec rnd): *P1, ssp, purl to 1 st before marker, p2tog, p1; rep from * around—93 (101, 109, 117) sts.

Cont to make additional decreases at markers as follows:

Left Sleeve: Dec 1 st each side every 3rd rnd 3 (4, 5, 5) more times.

Front: Dec 1 st each side every 3rd rnd 3 (3, 3, 4) more times.

Right Sleeve: Dec 1 st each side every 3rd rnd 3 (4, 5, 5) more times.

Back: Dec 1 st each side every 3rd rnd 3 (3, 3, 4) more times.

AT THE SAME TIME, after two Armhole shapings are complete, work short-row Neck shaping as follows:

Work to 3 sts from left Center Neck, wrap and turn. Work to 3 sts from right Center Neck, wrap and turn. Work to 6 sts from left Center Neck, wrap and turn. Work to 3 sts from right Center Neck, wrap and turn.

Continue on all sts. When all shaping is complete, 69 (73, 77, 81) sts rem.

Next rnd: P2tog, p1, *k2, p2; rep from *. Work 7 more rows in k2, p2 rib as established.

Bind off. Sew Sleeve seams. Graft Underarm join. Weave in ends.

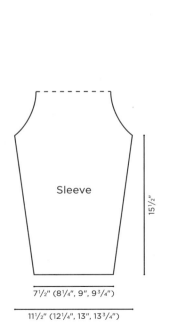

Sleeve

15½"

7½" (8¼", 9", 9¾")

11½" (12¼", 13", 13¾")

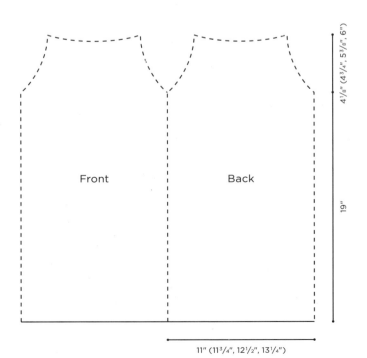

Front

Back

4⅛" (4¾", 5⅜", 6")

19"

11" (11¾", 12½", 13¼")

feather scarf

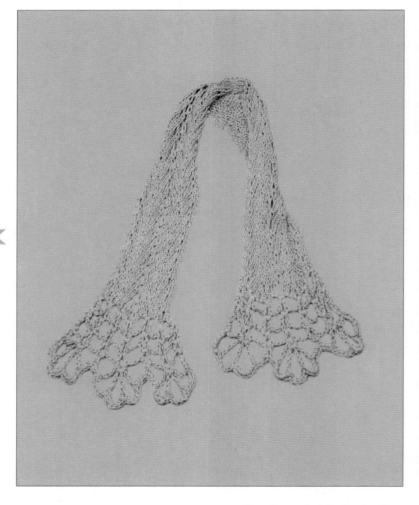

ONE SIZE

KNITTED MEASUREMENTS
8" x 56" (20x142cm)

MATERIALS
5 (6, 6) skeins of Twinkle Handknits Cruise (70% silk, 30% cotton; 120 yd/112 m per 50 g ball) in Capri *or* 552 yd/503 m of any DK weight yarn in the color of your choice

US size 17 (12.75mm) knitting needles or size to obtain gauge

Size N/15 (10mm) crochet hook

GAUGE
10 sts and 12 ½ rows = 4" (10cm) in St st on size 17 needles, holding 4 strands together. Exact gauge is not crucial in this project.

NOTE
Scarf is knit holding 4 strands together throughout.

SPECIAL STITCHES
ch: Chain stitch
dc: Double crochet
dtr: Double treble crochet
k2tog: Knit 2 together
sc: Single crochet
SSK: Slip, slip, knit 2 together
yo: Yarn over

FEATHER PATTERN

ROW 1 (RS): ★K1, yo, k2, ssk, k2tog, k2, yo; rep from ★.

ROW 2: Purl.

ROW 3: ★Yo, k2, ssk, k2tog, k2, yo, k1; rep from ★.

ROW 4: Purl.

FEATHER STITCH PATTERN

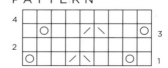

	= K on RS, P on WS
O	= yo
\	= SSK
/	= K2tog

Rep Rows 1–4 for Feather Pattern.

SCARF
CO 22 sts.

K2, work Feather Pattern across next 18 sts, k2.

Keeping first and last 2 sts in garter st (knit every row), work Feather Pattern across center 18 sts for 100 rows. Scarf measures approx 42" (106.5cm). BO loosely.

LACE TRIM
With crochet hook and RS facing, join yarn at corner of cast-on edge.

ROW 1: Ch-3, dc in same sp, ★ch-3, sk 2 sts, (dc, ch-2, dc) in next st, ch-3, sk 3 sts (dc, ch-2, dc) in next st; rep from ★ across, ending last rep 2 dc in last st.

ROWS 2-3: Ch-3, dc in same sp, ch-3 ★(dc, ch-2, dc) in next ch-2 sp, ch-3; rep from ★ across, 2 dc in top of ch-3 of previous row.

ROW 4: Ch-1, sc in same st, ★ch-2, [(dtr, ch 5) 3 times, dtr] in next ch-2 sp, ch-2, sc in next ch-2 sp; rep from ★, end last rep sc in top of ch-3 of previous row.

ROW 5: Ch-1, 3 sc in ch-2 sp, ★(6 sc in next ch-5 sp) 3 times, (1 sc in next ch-2 sp) 2 times; rep from ★, end last rep 3 sc in last ch-2 sp.

Fasten off.

Repeat lace trim on bound-off edge.

CROCHET ENDS

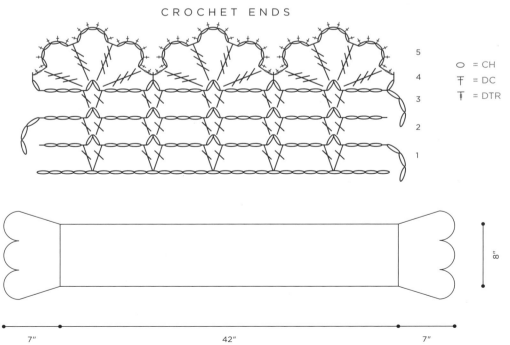

○ = CH
⊤ = DC
⊤ = DTR

5
4
3
2
1

8"

7"   42"   7"

convertible cardigan

SIZES S (M, L)

KNITTED MEASUREMENTS
Bust: 31½" (33¼", 35")
Front Finished Length (excluding collar):
24" (24⅝", 25½")

MATERIALS:
25 (29, 33) skeins of Twinkle Handknits
Cruise (70% silk, 30% cotton; 109 yds/ 100
m per 50g skein) in Indigo *or* 2242 yds/
2040 m of any DK yarn

US sizes 13 (9 mm) and 15 (10 mm) 24"
circular needles

Stitch markers

Stitch holders

Twelve 1" (2.5 cm) buttons

GAUGE
Knitting 4 strands together, 10 sts and 12½
rows = 4" (10 cm) in St st on size 15 (10
mm) needles

NOTE
This sweater is worked back and forth on a
circular needle with four strands held
together throughout. Sleeves are knit to the
underarm first. Body is worked in one piece
to the underarm, then sleeves are joined to
body. Make all pockets and sleeves first.

LOWER POCKETS
(MAKE 4)
With larger needles, cast on 14 sts. Work 12 rows St st.

Place sts on holder.

UPPER POCKETS
(MAKE 2)
With larger needles, cast on 12 sts. Work 12 rows in St st.

Place sts on holder.

SLEEVE
(MAKE 2)
With smaller needles, cast on 17 sts. Row 1: K1, *k2, p2; rep from
*. Work 11 more rows in k2, p2 rib as established, increasing 4 sts
evenly across last row—21 sts. Change to larger needles and work
10 (8, 8) rows stockinette stitch, beg with a knit row. Next Row
(Inc Row): K1, m1, knit to last st, m1, k1. Rep Inc Row every 8th
row 4 (4, 1) times and every 6th row 0 (1, 5) times—31 (33, 35)
sts. Work even until sleeve measures 19½" (49.5 cm). Bind off 2 sts
at beg of next 2 rows—27 (29, 31) sts. Place sts on holder.

BODY
With smaller needles, cast on 84 (88, 92) sts. Row 1 (right side):
*K1, p1; rep from * across. Work 11 more rows in k1, p1 rib as
established.

Change to larger needles and stockinette stitch.

ROW 1: K20 (21, 22), pm, k44 (46, 48), pm, knit to end.

Work even 5 (5, 7) more rows. Next row (Dec Row): Knit to 3 sts
before marker, k2tog, k1, sl marker, k1, ssk, rep from * once, knit
to end. Repeat Dec Row every 6th row 3 more times AT THE
SAME TIME, when 12 rows of stockinette stitch are complete,
join pockets as follows:

K2, place next 14 pocket sts on holder and hold at front of work,
knit 14 Lower Pocket sts from holder, knit to 16 sts from end,
place next 14 pocket sts on holder and hold at front of work, knit
14 Lower Pocket sts from holder, k2—68 (72, 76) sts remain after
side decreases are complete.

Work even 5 rows. Next row (Inc Row): Knit to 1 st before
marker, m1, k1, sl marker, k1, m1; rep from * once, knit to end.
Repeat Inc Row every 8th row once—76 (80, 84) sts. Work even
until Body measures approximately 18½" (47 cm), ending with a
wrong side row.

DIVIDE BODY AND JOIN POCKET

K2, place next 12 pocket sts on holder and hold at front of work, k12 sts from one Upper Pocket, k2 (3, 4) sts, bind off 4 sts, k36 (38, 40) Back sts, bind off 4, knit to last 14 sts, place next 12 pocket sts on holder and hold at front of work, k12 sts from remaining Upper Pocket, k2 (3, 4).

JOIN SLEEVES

Wrong side facing, purl Left Front sts, pm, p27 (29, 31) Sleeve sts from holder, pm, purl Back sts, pm, p 27 (29, 31) sts Sleeve sts from holder, pm, purl Right Front sts—122 (130, 138) sts.

Work even 4 rows. Next row (Dec Row): Knit to 3 sts before marker, k2tog, k1, sl marker, k1, ssk; rep from * three times, knit to end. Rep Dec Row every right side row 6 times, ending with a wrong side row—66 (74, 82) sts.

NECK SHAPING AND BACK SHAPING

Next row: Bind off 8 sts, knit to second marker, k1, ssk, knit to 3 sts before next marker, k2tog, knit to end. Bind off 8 sts at beg of next row and 7 sts at beg of next 2 rows—34 (42, 50) sts.

NECK BAND

Change to smaller needles. Row 1 sts (right side): K2, *p2, k2; rep from * across. Work 37 more rows in k2, p2 rib as established. Bind off loosely.

BUTTON BAND

Right side facing, with smaller needles, pick up and knit 81 (83, 85) sts from Left Front edge. Row 1 (right side): K1, *p1, k1; rep from *. Work 7 more rows in k1, p1 rib as established. Bind off.

BUTTONHOLE BAND

Place markers on Right Front edge for 5 buttonholes, the first and last 1" (2.5 cm) from the neck and lower edges, and 10 evenly spaced between.

Right side facing, with smaller needles, pick up and knit 81 (83, 85) sts along edge. Row 1 (right side): K1, *p1, k1; rep from *. Work 1 more row in k1, p1 rib. Next row (Buttonhole row): Cont in established rib, work (yo, k2tog) or (yo, p2tog) buttonholes at each mark. Work 3 more rows in established rib. Bind off.

Sew Sleeve and seams. Weave underarm seams. Sew pocket linings to sweater.

Pocket flap: Place pocket sts on smaller needle and work 4 rows k1, p1 rib. Bind off. Sew sides of pocket flap to sweater. Repeat for other pockets.

Sew one button on wrong side of buttonband opposite top buttonhole. Sew remaining buttons on right side of buttonband opposite buttonholes.

Weave in ends.

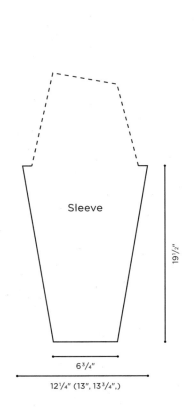

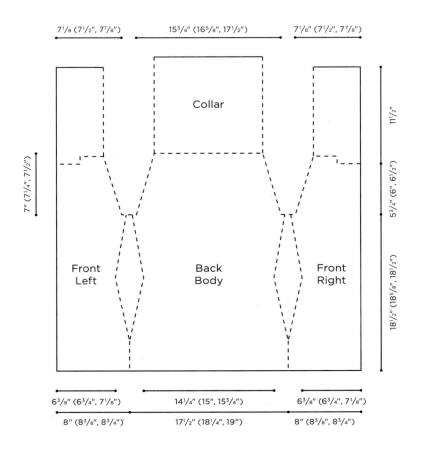

night
on
the
town

incredible skirt

SIZE
One size

KNITTED MEASUREMENTS
Short version: 24" (61cm) waist X 24" (61cm) length
Long version: 24" (61cm) waist X 42" (106.5cm) length

MATERIALS
Short version: 1 skein of Classic Elite Le Gran Mohair (76.5% mohair, 17.5% wool, 6% wool; 90 yd/82m) per 1.5 oz skein in #6516 Natural (A); 1 skein of Reyold's Lopi (100% Icelandic Wool; 100 yd/91.5m per 100 g skein) in each of the following colors: #54 Pale Undyed, #307 Rose, #47 Happy Red, and #116 Garnet.

Long version: 1 skein of Classic Elite Le Gran Mohair (76.5% mohair, 17.5% wool, 6% wool; 90 yd/82m) per 1.5 oz skein in #6516 Natural (A);1 skein of Reyold's Lopi (100% Icelandic Wool; 100 yd/91.5m per 100 g skein) in each of the following colors: #54 Pale Undyed, #432 Grape Heather, #57 Medium Grey, #9986 Slate, and #59 Black.

US size 13 (9mm) and 15 (10mm) 24" circular needles

US size 17 (12.75mm) and 19 (15mm) 29" circular needles

½" (1.25 cm) elastic for waistband (long version)

GAUGE
10 sts and 12½ rows in St st on size 15 needles.

NOTES
Color changes take place gradually, moving from lighter to darker at the waist. To make the color changes smoothly, alternate yarn color by carrying the yarn across the back for no more than 5–6 sts. Use the charts at right as a guide to approximate the number of stitches of each color on the round.

SHORT SHIRT

With largest needles and A, CO 156 sts. Pm to indicate beginning of rnd. Join, being careful not to twist stitches.

RNDS 1–4: *K1, p1; rep from *.

RND 5: *K26, pm; rep from *, ending with last marker at end of rnd.

Cont in St st (knit every rnd), following the color chart at right, and at the same time make decreases as follows:

RND 12 (DEC RND): *K1, ssk, k to 3 sts before marker, k2tog, k1; rep from *—144 sts.

RND 17: Rep Dec Rnd—132 sts.

RND 22: Rep Dec Rnd—120 sts.

RND 32: Rep Dec Rnd—108 sts.

RND 37: Rep Dec Rnd—96 sts.

RND 42: Rep Dec Rnd—84 sts.

RND 47: Rep Dec Rnd—72 sts.

RND 52: Rep Dec Rnd—60 sts.

RNDS 53–57: *K1, p1; rep from *. BO loosely. Weave in ends.

LONG SKIRT

With largest needles and A, CO 300 sts. Pm to indicate beginning of rnd. Join, being careful not to twist stitches.

RNDS 1–4: *K1, p1; rep from *.

RND 5: *K50, pm; rep from *, ending with last marker at end of rnd.

Cont in St st (knit every rnd), following chart at right, and at the same time make decreases as follows:

RND 12 (DEC RND): *K1, ssk, k to 3 sts before marker, k2tog, k1; rep from *—288 sts.

RND 23: Rep Dec Rnd—276 sts.

RND 31: Rep Dec Rnd—264 sts.

RND 39: Rep Dec Rnd—252 sts.

LONG VERSION

YARN/ RND	MOHAIR	PALE UNDYED	GRAPE HEATHR	MEDIUM GREY	SLATE	BLACK	NDLE SIZE	#OF STS
R 1-6	entire rnd						#17	300 st
R 7-8	the rest	50 st						
R 9-10	the rest	80 st						
R 11	the rest	110 st						
R 12	the rest	110 st	188 st					
R 13-14	the rest	140 st						
R 15-16	the rest	170 st						
R 17-18	the rest	200 st						
R 19-20	the rest	230						
R 21-22		entire rnd						
* R 23		entire rnd						276 st
R 24		entire rnd						
R 25		entire rnd					#15	
R 26		entire rnd						
R 27-28		the rest	50 st					
R 29-30		the rest	75 st					
* R 31		the rest	100 st					264 st
R 32		the rest	100 st					
R 33-34		the rest	125 st					
R 35-36		the rest	150 st					
R 37-38		the rest	175 st					
* R 39		the rest	200 st					252 st
R 40		the rest	200 st					
R 41-46			entire rnd					
* R 47			the rest	50 st				240 st
R 48			the rest	50 st				
R 49-51			the rest	75 st				
R 52-54			the rest	100 st				
R 55			the rest	135 st				
R 56-57			the rest	135 st				
R 58-60			the rest	165 st				
R 61-62				entire rnd				
* R 63				entire rnd				216 st
R 64-66				entire rnd				
* R 71				the rest	40 st			204 st
R 72				the rest	40 st			
R 73-74				the rest	70 st			
R 75-76				the rest	100 st			
R 77-78				the rest	130 st			
* R 79				the rest	155 st			192 st
R 80				the rest	155 st			
R 81-85					entire rnd			
* R 86					entire rnd			180 st
R 87-88					the rest	45 st		
R 89-90					the rest	60 st		
R 91-92					the rest	75 st		
* R 93					the rest	75 st		168 st
R 94					the rest	75 st		
R 95-97					the rest	100 st		
R 98-99					the rest	125 st		
* R 100					the rest	125 st		156 st
R 101-103						entire rnd		
R 104						entire rnd	#13	
R 105-6						entire rnd		
* R 107						entire rnd		144 st
R 108-13						entire rnd		
* R 114						entire rnd		72 st
R 115-26						entire rnd		

* Decrease round

SHORT VERSION

YARN/ RND	MOHAIR	PALE UNDYED	ROSE	HAPPY RED	GARNET	NDLE SIZE	#OF STS
R 1-8	entire rnd					#17	156
R 9	the rest	8 st					
R 10	the rest	16 st					
R 11	the rest	35 st					
* R 12	the rest	70 st				#15	144 st
R 13	the rest	120 st					
R 14-16		entire rnd					
* R 17		entire rnd					132 st
R 18		the rest	10 st				
R 19-20		the rest	20 st				
R 21		the rest	30 st				
* R 22		the rest	45 st				120 st
R 23		the rest	60 st				
R 24		the rest	70 st				
R 25		the rest	80 st				
R 26		the rest	90 st				
R 27		the rest	100 st				
R 28			entire rnd				
R 29			the rest	10 st			
R 30			the rest	15 st			
R 31			the rest	20 st			
* R 32			the rest	25 st			108 st
R 33-34			the rest	40 st			
R 35			the rest	55 st			
R 36			the rest	70 st			
* R 37			the rest	85 st			96 st
R 38-39			the rest	85 sts			
R 40				entire rnd			
R 41				the rest	7 st		
* R 42				the rest	15 st		84 st
R 43				the rest	15 st		
R 44-46				the rest	20 st		
* R 47				the rest	25 st		72 st
R 48				the rest	30 st		
R 49-50				the rest	35 st		
R 51				the rest	40 st		
* R 52				the rest	45 st	#13	60 st
R 53				the rest	50 st		
R 54-66				the rest	all rnds		

* Decrease round

INCREDIBLE SKIRT (LONG)

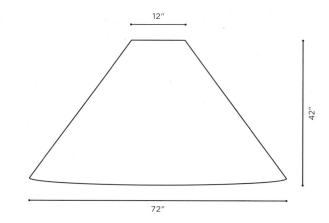

12"

42"

72"

INCREDIBLE SKIRT (SHORT)

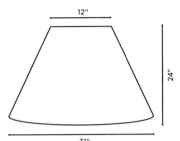

12"

24"

31"

RND 47: Rep Dec Rnd—240 sts.

RND 55: Rep Dec Rnd—228 sts.

RND 63: Rep Dec Rnd—216 sts.

RND 71: Rep Dec Rnd—204 sts.

RND 79: Rep Dec Rnd—192 sts.

RND 86: Rep Dec Rnd—180 sts.

RND 93: Rep Dec Rnd—168 sts.

RND 100: Rep Dec Rnd—156 sts.

RND 107: Rep Dec Rnd—104 sts.

RND 114: (K2tog) around—72 sts.

RNDS 115–126: With F, *k1, p1; rep from *. BO loosely. Cut elastic to fit Waist. Sew ends of elastic together. Place elastic at Waist. Fold ribbing over and sew, encasing elastic.

princess capelet

ONE SIZE

KNITTED MEASUREMENTS
Bust: 30" (76cm)
Front Length (excluding collar): 15" (38cm)

MATERIALS
4 (5, 5) skeins of twinke Handknits Soft Chunky (100% merino wool; 83 yd/77 m per 200 g skein) in Lilac *or* 302 yd/276 m of any super bulky weight yarn in the color of your choice

US size 19 (15 mm) 29" (73.5cm) circular needles

15mm crochet hook

Waste yarn for stitch holder

GAUGE
6½ sts and 11¼" (28.5cm) rows = 4" (10cm) in seed st on size 19 needles

NOTES
Entire piece is worked in seed stitch. Use k2tog or p2tog decreases, as necessary, to maintain stitch pattern. Sleeves are knit first. Body is knit in one piece to underarms, then sleeves are joined to body and worked together.

SPECIAL STITCHES
Decrease: (K2tog) or (P2tog), as necessary, to maintain stitch pattern
K1f&b: Knit into the front and back of next st

SEED STITCH
ROW/RND 1: *K1, p1; rep from *.

ROW/RND 2: Purl the knit sts and knit the purl sts.

Rep Row/Rnd 2 for pattern.

SLEEVES
(MAKE 2)
CO 34 sts. Work 2 rows in seed st, placing marker at center point of Sleeve on 2nd row.

Next row (Dec Row): Work to 2 sts before marker, dec, sl marker, dec, work to end of

row. Maintaining st pattern, rep Dec Row every 3rd row 6 more times—20 sts. Work even 1 row. Bind off 2 sts at beg of next 2 rows. Place sts on holder.

BODY

CO 42 sts. Work 2 rows seed st. Next row (Inc Row): K1f&b, work to last st, k1f&b. Repeat Inc Row every other row 5 more times, bringing new sts into pattern—54 sts. Work even until 22 rows are complete, ending with a WS row. Body measures approx 7¾" (19.5cm).

Divide body (RS): Work in established pattern across 12 Right Front sts, BO next 4 sts, pattern across 22 Back sts, BO next 4 sts, pattern across remaining 12 Left Front sts.

Join sleeves (WS): Pattern across Left Front sts, pm, pattern across Left Sleeve sts, pm, pattern across Back sts, pm, pattern across Right Sleeve sts, pm, pattern across Right Front sts—78 sts.

Next row (Dec Row): ★Work in pattern to 2 sts before marker, dec, sl marker, dec; rep from ★ across. Rep Dec Row every 3 rows 5 more times—30 sts. Work even 2 rows.

Next row (RS): BO 4 sts, work to second marker, sl marker, dec, work to 2 sts before next marker, dec, sl marker, work to end of row. BO 4 sts at beg of next row. BO 3 sts at beg of next two rows—14 sts. Cut yarn.

COLLAR

With RS facing, pick up and knit 7 sts along Right Front neck, work in established seed st across 12 right sleeve and Back Neck and Left Sleeve sts, and 7 sts along Left Front Neck—26 sts. Work 5 rows even in seed st.

Decrease 1 st each side every other row 3 times—20 sts. Work 1 row even. Bind off.

FINISHING

With RS facing, attach yarn to lower Underarm edge. With crochet hook, sl st around entire edge of garment, including Collar, placing hook into every st around and into every other row around. Fasten off. Repeat sl st border for lower Sleeve edges.

Make 2 pom-poms 4" (10cm) in diameter (see page 75). With crochet hook, crochet 2 chains 12" (30cm) long. Attach pom-pom onto the end of each chain, and sew the chain to the corner of Neck.

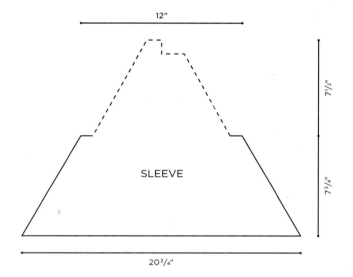

12"

7½"

7¾"

SLEEVE

20¾"

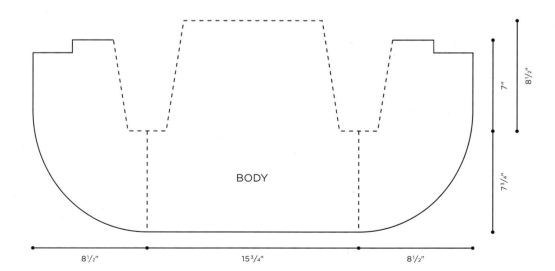

7"

8½"

7¾"

BODY

8½"   15¾"   8½"

mini bolero

PICOT BORDER PATTERN
Sc in next 2 sc, *ch 3, sc in same st, sc in next 3 sc; rep from *, ending last rep sc in last 2 sc.

BODY
CO 74 (78, 82) sts. Beg with a knit row, work even in St st for 8 (8, 10) rows.

DIVIDE FOR ARMHOLES
(RS) K18 (19, 20) Right Front sts, place on holder, bind off next 2 sts, k36 (38, 40) Back sts, place remaining 20 (21, 22) Left Front sts on holder.

Working on Back sts only, purl 1 row. BO 1 st at beg of next 2 rows. Work even 14 (16, 16) more rows, ending with a WS row.

SHOULDER SHAPING
BO 2 sts at beg of next 8 rows. BO rem 18 (20, 22) sts.

RIGHT FRONT
Place Right Front sts on needle. Beg with WS, work 2 rows even. BO 1 st at beg of next row. Work even 14 more rows, ending with a WS row.

NECK SHAPING
At Neck edge, BO 3 sts 1 (1, 2) times, 2 sts (1, 1, 0) times, and 1 st 3 (4, 4) times. Bind off rem 9 sts.

LEFT FRONT
Place rem 20 (21, 22) Left Front sts on needle. With RS facing, BO 2 sts, knit to end. BO 1 st at Armhole edge once. Work even until Left Front measures same as Right Front to Neck shaping, ending with a RS row.

NECK SHAPING
At Neck edge, BO 3 sts 1 (1, 2) times, 2 sts (1, 1, 0) times, and 1 st 3 (4, 4) times. BO rem 9 sts.

SLEEVE

(MAKE 2)

CO 19 sts. Beg with a knit row, work even in St st for 4 rows.
Next row (Inc Row): K1, m1, knit to last st, m1, k1. Rep Inc Row
every 10th (8th, 6th) row 4 (5, 3) times, then every 8th row 0 (0,
3) times—29 (31, 33) sts.

Work even until Sleeve measures 17½" (44.5cm), ending with a
WS row.

CAP SHAPING

Dec Row: K1, ssk, k to last 3 sts, k2tog, k1. Purl one row. Rep
Dec Row every other row 8 more times—11 (13, 15) sts. Bind off.

FINISHING

Sew Front Shoulders to sloped portion of Back Shoulders. Set in
Sleeves and sew Sleeve seams.

SLEEVE EDGING

With crochet hook and RS facing, join yarn at lower edge of
Sleeve. Ch-1, sc into each cast-on st, join with sl st—19 sc. Work
Picot Border Pattern. Fasten off.

BODY EDGING

With crochet hook and RS facing, join yarn at lower edge and
work around entire outside edge of cardigan as follows:

Ch-1, work 1 rnd sc evenly around, placing 2 sc into each corner
st, join with sl st to beg ch-1. Work Picot Border Pattern. Fasten
off.

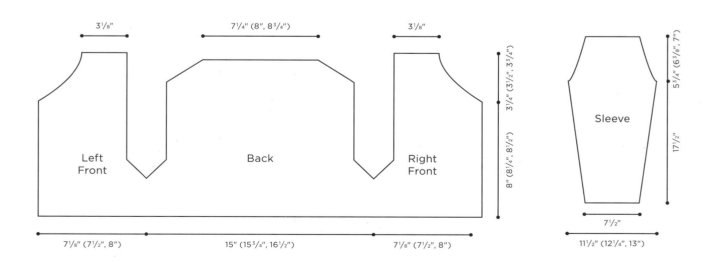

marilyn jacket

SIZES S (M, L)

FINISHED MEASUREMENTS
Bust: approx 32" (81cm)
Length: 19" (21", 22") [49 (50, 51.5cm)]

MATERIALS
2 (3, 3) skeins of Twinkle Handknits Soft
Chunky (100% merino wool; 83 yd/77 m
per 200 g skein) in Cream (A); 3 (3, 4)
skeins in Black (B) *or* 164 yd/150m of any
super bulky weight yarn in (A) color or the
color of your choice; 200 yd/183 m of any
super weight yarn in (B) color or the color
of your choice

US size 17 (10mm) and 19 (12.75mm) 24"
circular needles

Stitch holder

GAUGE
One 19-stitch full-stitch pattern repeat =
10" on size 19 needles.

NOTES
This sweater is worked back and forth on a
circular needle. Stitch counts do not change
for the different sizes, but row counts
increase incrementally. Carry yarn not being
used loosely up side.

SPECIAL STITCHES
k2tog: Knit 2 together
SSK: Slip, slip knit 2 together
yo: Yarn over

RIGHT FRONT PATTERN
(OVER 10 STS)
ROW 1: With A, knit.

ROW 2: Purl.

ROW 3: K1, (yo, k1) 3 times, (ssk) 3 times.

ROW 4: Knit.

ROWS 5-8: With B, repeat Rows 1–4.

Rep Rows 1–8 for pattern.

LEFT FRONT PATTERN
(OVER 10 STS)
ROW 1: With A, Knit.

ROW 2: Purl.

ROW 3: (K2tog) 3 times, (k1, yo) 3 times,
k1.

ROW 4: Knit.

ROWS 5-8: With B, repeat Rows 1–4.

Rep Rows 1–8 for pattern.

FULL STITCH PATTERN
(MULT OF 19 + 1)
ROW 1 (RS): Knit.

ROW 2: Purl.

ROW 3: *K1, (yo, k1) 3 times, (ssk) 3 times,
(k2tog) 3 times, (k1, yo) 3 times; rep from
*, k1.

ROW 4: Knit.

RIGHT FRONT

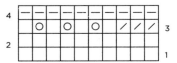

☐ = K on RS, P on WS
O = yo
\ = SSK
⊟ = P on RS, K on WS
/ = K2tog

LEFT FRONT

FULL STITCH PATTERN

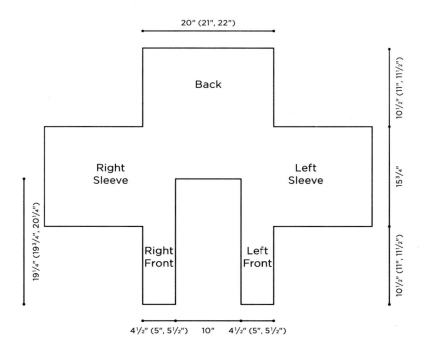

RIGHT FRONT

With A, CO 10 sts. Work Right Front stitch pattern for 24 (28, 32) rows. Begin Sleeve: Work in pattern across 10 sts, CO 29 sts— 39 sts.

P29, work in pattern across rem 10 sts.

Beg with Row 3 of Full Stitch Pattern, work Full Stitch Pattern across all sts for 18 more rows, ending with a WS row. Place sts on holder.

LEFT FRONT

With A, cast on 10 sts. Work Left Front st pattern for 24 (28, 32) rows. With A (B, A), CO 29 sts at end of Row 24 (28, 32).

ROW 25 (29, 33): K29, work in pattern across rem 10 sts (knit).

ROW 26 (30, 34): Work in pattern across 10 sts (purl), purl to end.

Beg with Row 3 of Full Stitch Pattern, work Full Stitch Pattern across all sts for 18 more rows.

JOIN FRONTS

With RS facing, work Full Stitch Pattern across Left Front sts (knit), CO 18 sts, work Full Stitch Pattern across Right Front sts (knit)—96 sts. Cont in pattern as established for 15 more rows, ending with a WS row. K29 sleeve sts, pattern across rem sts.

P29, pattern across back sts, p29.

BO 29 sts at beg of next two rows. Cont in established pattern on Back sts only for 24 (38, 32) more rows, ending with 4 rows of A.

FINISHING

Block sweater to match schematic below.

With RS facing, join yarn at lower Right Front edge and pick up 2 sts from every 3 rows along Right Front edge, 1 st from each st across Back Neck, and 2 sts from every 3 rows along left front edge. Work 6 rows k1, p1 rib. BO.

Fold garment in half and seam Sleeve and side seams.

evening shell

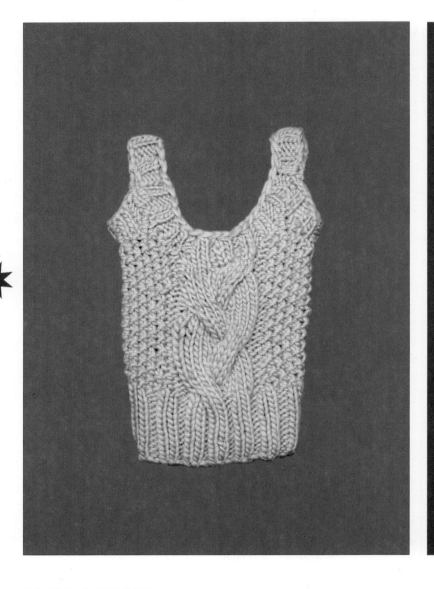

SIZES S (M, L)

FINISHED MEASUREMENTS
Bust: 25" (27½", 30") [63.5 (70, 76)cm]
Length (Long version): 26¼" (26¾", 27¼")
[66.5 (68, 69)cm]
Length (Short version): 20½" (21", 21½")
[52 (53, 54.5)cm]

MATERIALS
2 (3, 3) skeins of Twinkle Handknits Soft
Chunky (100% merino wool; 83 yd/77 m
per 200 g skein) in Lilac *or* 164 yd/150 m of
any super bulky weight yarn in the color of
your choice

US size 17 (12.75mm) and 19 (15mm) 24"
(61cm) circular needles

Size Q (15mm) crochet hook

GAUGE
6½ sts and 11¼ rows= 4" (10cm) in seed st
on size 19 needles

NOTES
Body is knit in one piece to armhole and
neck shaping.
When pattern calls for a decrease, use a
(k2tog) or (p2tog) decrease, as needed, to
maintain seed stitch pattern.

SPECIAL STITCHES
C8L (Cable 8 left): Slip next 4 sts to cable
needle and hold in front of work, k4, k4
from cable needle
C8R (cable 8 right): Slip next 4 sts to cable
needle and hold in back of work, k4, k4
from cable needle

CABLE PATTERN
(OVER 16 STS)

ROW 1 (RIGHT SIDE): P2, k12, p2.

ROW 2 AND ALL WS ROWS: K2, p12, k2.

ROW 3: P2, k4, C8R, p2.

ROWS 5 AND 7: P2, k12, p2.

ROW 9: P2, C8L, k4, p2.

ROW 11: P2, k12, p2.

ROW 12: K2, p12, k2.

Rep Rows 1–12.

CABLE PATTERN

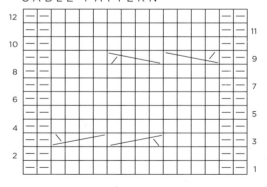

☐ = P on RS, K on WS

☐ = K on RS, P on WS

= C8L

= C8R

SEED STITCH

RND 1: *K1, p1; rep from * (ending k1, if necessary, for st multiple).

RND 2: Purl the knit sts and knit the purl sts.

Rep Rnd 2.

SHORT VERSION

With smaller needles, CO 48 (52, 56) sts. Pm to indicate beginning of rnd. Join, being careful not to twist stitches. *K2, p2; rep from *. Work 11 more rnds in k2, p2 rib as established. Change to larger needles.

RND 1: Work seed st across 22 (24, 26) Back sts, pm to indicate left Underarm, work Cable Pattern over next 16 sts, pm, work seed st across rem 5 (6, 7) sts.

Cont in established patterns, work 3 rnds even. Next rnd (Dec Rnd): Pattern to 2 sts before marker, dec, sl marker, work Cable Pattern, sl marker, dec, pattern to end. Work 3 rnds even. Rep Dec Rnd—44 (48, 52) sts. Work 7 rnds even. Next rnd (Inc Rnd): Pattern to first cable marker, m1, sl marker, work Cable Pattern, sl marker, m1, pattern across rem sts—46 (50, 54) sts. Work even 6 rnds, ending last rnd 1 st before end of rnd.

ARMHOLE AND NECK SHAPING

Right Back Shoulder: BO 2 sts, work seed st across next 5 (6, 7) sts, turn.

BO 2 sts at beg of next row, work to end. [Size L only: Work even 1 row. BO 1 st at beg of next row]—3 (4, 4) sts. Work even 4 (4, 2) rows. BO 1 st at beg of next 2 rows—1 (2, 2) sts. Work 2 rows even. Bind off.

Left Back Shoulder: With RS facing, rejoin yarn at back neck, BO next 10 sts, work seed st across next 5 (6, 7) sts, turn.

Work even 1 row. BO 2 sts at beg of next row. [Size L only: BO 1 st at beg of row, work to end.]

Work 3 (3, 1) rows even. BO 1 st at beg of next 2 rows. Work 3 rows even—1 (2, 2) sts. Bind off.

Left Front Shoulder: With RS facing, rejoin yarn at left Underarm, BO 2 sts, work seed st across next 5 (6, 7) sts, turn. BO 2 sts at beg of next row. [Size L only: BO 1 st at beg of row, work to end.]

Work 3, (3, 2) rows even. BO 1 st at beg of next 2 rows—1 (2, 2) sts. Work 3 rows even. Bind off.

Right Front Shoulder: With RS facing, rejoin yarn at Front Neck, BO 12 sts, work seed st across next 5 (6, 7) sts, turn. Work 1 row even. BO 2 sts at beg of next row. [Size L only: BO1 st at beg of next row.] Work 3 (3, 2) rows even. BO 1 st at beg of next 2 rows. Work 2 rows even. Bind off.

ARMBANDS

With RS facing, with smaller needles, pick up 14 sts along Armhole edge. Row 1 (WS): P2, *k2, p2; rep from *. Work 2 more rows k2, p2 rib as established. Bind off. Repeat for other Armband.

NECKBAND

With RS facing, with smaller needles, pick up 30 (32, 34) sts around Front Neck edge and side of Armband, CO 12 sts for Shoulder, pick up 30 (32, 34) sts around side of Armband and Back Neck edge, CO 12 sts for Shoulder—84 (88, 92) sts. Begin working in the round as follows:

RNDS 1–4: *K2, p2; rep from *. Bind off.

LONG VERSION

With smaller needles, CO 48 (52, 56) sts. Pm to indicate beginning of rnd. Join, being careful not to twist stitches. *K2, p2; rep from *. Work 11 more rnds in k2, p2 rib as established. Change to larger needles.

RND 1: Work seed st across 22 (24, 26) Back sts, pm to indicate left Underarm, work seed st across next 5 (6, 7) sts, pm, work Cable Pattern over next 16 sts, pm, work seed st across rem 5 (6, 7) sts. Cont in established patterns, work even 19 rnds. Next rnd (Dec Rnd): Pattern to 2 sts before marker, dec, work Cable Pattern, dec, pattern to end. Work 3 rounds even. Rep Dec Rnd—44 (48, 52) sts. Work 7 rnds even. Next rnd (Inc Rnd): Pattern to first cable marker, m1, sl marker, work Cable Pattern, sl marker, m1, pattern across rem sts—46 (50, 54) sts. Work even 6 rnds, ending last rnd 1 st before end of rnd.

Work shaping and finish as for short version.

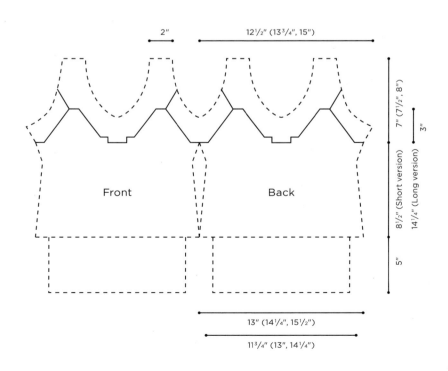

mohair shrug

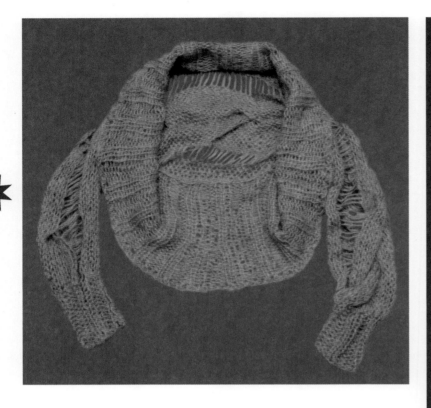

SIZES S (M, L)

KNITTED MEASUREMENTS
Bust: 30" (31½", 33") [76 (80, 84)cm]

MATERIALS
2 (3, 3) skeins of Twinkle Handknit Kids
Mohair (25% Wool, 25% Mohair, 50%
Acrylic; 310 yd/290 m per 50 g skein) in
Dusty Rose *or* Silver Lavender *or* 633
yd/577 m of any fine mohair yarn in the
color of your choice

US size 17 (12.75mm) and 19 (15mm)
needles 24" (61cm) circular needles.

Size Q (15mm) crochet hook

GAUGE
8 sts and 14 rows = 4" (10cm) in k2, p2 rib
on size 17 needles

SPECIAL STITCHES
C12L (Cable 12 left): Slip next 6 sts to cable
needle and hold in front of work, k6, 6 from
cable needle
C12R (Cable 12 right): Slip next 6 sts to
cable needle and hold in back of work, k6,
k6 from cable needle

MOHAIR CABLE PATTERN
(OVER 18 STS)
ROW 1 (RS): Knit.

ROW 2 AND ALL WS ROWS: Purl.

ROW 3: K6, C12L.

ROWS 5, 7, AND 9: Knit.

ROW 11: C12R, k6.

ROWS 13 AND 15: Knit.

ROW 16: Purl.

Rep Rows 1–16 for Cable Pattern.

SHRUG
With larger needles, CO 24 (26, 28) sts.

ROW 1: K2 (3, 4), p1, work Mohair Cable Pattern over next 18 sts, p1, k2 (3, 4).

ROW 2: P2 (3, 4), k1, work Mohair Cable Pattern over next 18 sts, p1, k2 (3, 4).

Cont in established pattern until 104 rows are complete.

K 2 (3, 4) drop next st and allow it to ladder down to cast-on row,

MOHAIR CABLE PATTERN

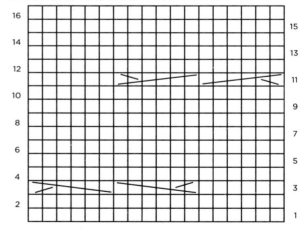

= K or RS, P on WS

= C12L

= C12R

BO 18, drop next st, BO rem 2 (3, 4).

CUFFS

With RS facing and smaller needles, pick up 17 sts along cast-on edge.

ROW 1: K1, *k2, p2; rep from *.

ROW 2: *K2, p2; rep from * to last st, p1.

Rep Rows 1 and 2 six times. BO loosely.

Make a second cuff from bound-off sts.

Fold shrug in half lengthwise. Seam cuffs and an additional 29 (28, 27) rows along each side toward center.

BODY OPENING

You now have a tube with an opening in the center. With RS facing and smaller needles, pick up and knit 34 (36, 38) Collar sts along one edge of center opening from seam to seam, pm, pick up and knit 42 (44, 46) lower hem sts to beg, pm to indicate beg of rnd—76 (80, 84) sts.

RND 1: *K2, p2; rep from *. Work 18 more rnds k2, p2 rib as established.

On next rnd, work to center back, (knit into the front and back of next stitch) twice, cont in established rib—78 (83, 86) sts. Bringing new sts into rib pattern, work 11 more rnds in k2, p2 rib as established.

Work loose crocheted bind-off.

CROCHETED BIND-OFF

Insert hook knitwise into first st on needle, yo and pull a loop through the st, allow st to drop off needle, *insert hook knitwise into next st on needle, yo and pull a loop through both st on needle and st on hook, allow st to drop off needle; rep from * across.

CENTER BACK RIB HEM

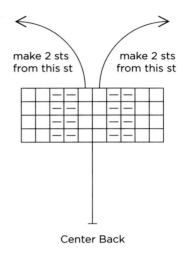

make 2 sts from this st   make 2 sts from this st

Center Back

☐ = K or RS, P on WS
⊟ = P on RS, K on WS

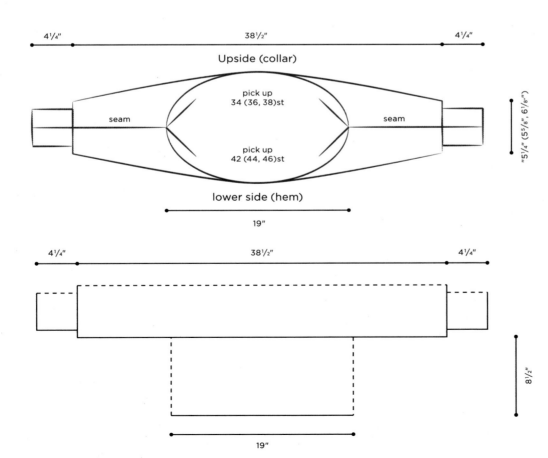

4¼"   38½"   4¼"

Upside (collar)

pick up 34 (36, 38)st

seam   seam

pick up 42 (44, 46)st

lower side (hem)

19"

5¼" (5⁵⁄₈", 6¹⁄₈")

4¼"   38½"   4¼"

8½"

19"

shop

the

town

twinkle hoodie

SIZES S, (M, L)

KNITTED MEASUREMENTS
Bust: 30" (32¼", 34½") [76 (82, 87.5)cm]
Front Length (excluding hood): 18½"
(19¼", 20") [47 (49, 51)cm]

MATERIALS
6 (7, 8) skeins of Twinkle Handknits Soft
Chunky in Gold (100% merino wool; 83
yd/77 m per 200 g skein) in White or
Canary or 467 yd/426 m of any super bulky
weight yarn in the color of your choice

US size 17 (12.75mm) and 19 (15mm) 24"
(61cm) circular needles

Size Q (15mm) crochet hook

Stitch markers

Stitch holders or waste yarn

Six 1¾" (4.5cm) buttons

GAUGE
6½ sts and 11¼ rows = 4" (10cm) in seed
st on size 19 needles.

NOTES
This sweater is worked back and forth on
a circular needle. Body is worked in one
piece to the underarm. Sleeves are knit
first and knit together with body from
armhole.

When decreasing, work (k2tog) or (p2tog)
decreases, as needed, to maintain stitch
pattern.

SEED STITCH
ROW 1: ★K1, p1; rep from ★.

ROW 2: Purl the knit sts and knit the purl sts.

Rep Row 2 for pattern.

RIGHT SLEEVE
With smaller needle, CO 17 sts.

ROW 1: K3, ★p2, k2; rep from ★.

Cont in k2, p2 rib as established for 5" (13cm). Change to larger
needles. Begin seed stitch, increasing 0 (2, 4) sts evenly across first
row—17 (19, 21) sts.

Work 12 rows even in seed stitch. Inc 1 st each side of next row—
19 (21, 23) sts. Work even until Sleeve measures 14½" (37cm),
ending with a WS row.

BO 2 sts at beg of next row and 3 sts at beg of following row.

Place rem 14 (16, 18) sts on waste yarn holder.

LEFT SLEEVE
Work as for Right Sleeve to bind-off row. BO 3 sts at beg of next
row and 2 sts at beg of following row. Place rem 14 (16, 18) sts on
waste yarn holder.

BODY
With smaller needles, CO 44 (48, 52) sts.

ROW 1 (RS): K3, ★p2, k2; rep from ★ to last st, k1.

Cont in established k2, p2 rib for 5" (13cm). End with a WS row.
Change to larger needles and seed stitch.

RIGHT FRONT POCKET
Work 7 (8, 9) sts in seed st for Right Front edge, place rem sts on
long holder or waste yarn. Work 2 rows. ★Dec 1 st at beg of next row,
work to end. Work 3 rows even. Rep from ★ two times—4 (5, 6) sts.

12 seed stitch rows are complete. Place sts on a second holder.

LEFT FRONT POCKET
Place last 7 (8, 9) sts from Left Front edge from holder onto needle. With WS facing, p1, (k1, p1) 3 times. Work 2 rows. *Dec 1 st at beg of next row, work to end. Work 3 rows even. Rep from *two times—4 (5, 6) sts. 12 seed stitch rows are complete. Place sts on a third holder.

With RS facing, pick up and knit 7 (8, 9) sts behind first 7 (8, 9) sts on Right Front Edge, work 15 (16, 17) sts from long holder, m1, work next 15 (16, 17) sts from holder, pick up and knit 7 (8, 9) sts behind last 7 (8, 9) sts on Left Front edge—45 (49, 53) sts. Work in seed st for 5 rows.

Dec Row (RS): *Work to 2 sts before marker, dec 1, sl marker, dec 1; rep from * once, work to end—43 (47, 51) sts. Work even 5 more rows. 12 seed st rows are complete.

JOIN POCKETS
Holding 4 (5, 6) Right Front Pocket sts on holder in front of body sts, keeping in pattern, *work together one st from Pocket and one st from Body; rep from * across Pocket sts, pattern across to second pocket, work left front Pocket sts together with body.

Work even 1 row.

Inc Row (RS): *Work to 1 st before marker, m1, sl marker, m1; rep from * once, work to end—45 (49, 53) sts.

Work even until body measures 12" (30.5cm) from beg.

DIVIDE BODY
Work 9 (10, 11) Right Front sts, BO next 4 sts, work 19 (21, 23) Back sts, BO next 4 sts, work 9 (10, 11) Left Front sts.

Join to Sleeves (WS): Pattern across Left Front sts, pm, pattern across Left Sleeve sts, pm, pattern across Back sts, pm, pattern across Right Sleeve sts, pm, pattern across Right Front sts—65 (73, 81) sts.

Work two rows even, then dec 1 st each side of markers next row. Work 2 rows even. Rep dec row every 3rd row 4 (5, 6) times—25 sts.

NECK SHAPING
Bind off 4 sts at each Neck edge once, and 2 sts twice. Leave rem 9 sts on needle, cut yarn.

HOOD
With RS facing, join yarn at Right Front neck. Pick up and knit 26 sts around Neck, including 9 Back Neck sts. Place marker at Center Back. Work even in established seed stitch until 24 rows are complete.

Dec Row: Work to 2 sts before marker, (dec) two times, work to end.

Work one row even. Rep decrease row every other row 5 times—14 sts. Bind off.

BANDS
Place a marker ½" (1cm) from lower Right Front edge and at Right Front Neck edge, and 4 markers evenly spaced between. With RS facing and smaller needles, pick up and knit 132 sts along Right Front, Hood, and Left Front (approx 3 sts from every 4 rows). Row 1 (RS): P3, *k2, p2; rep from * to last st, p1. Work even in k2, p2 rib, placing (yo, k2tog) or (yo, p2tog) buttonhole at each marker along right front on Row 3. Work until 6 ribbing rows are complete. Work crocheted bind-off along all sts.

POCKET FLAP
With smaller needles and RS facing, pick up 10 sts along one Pocket opening. Work 5 rows in k2, p2 rib. Work crocheted bind-off. Repeat for second Pocket Flap.

Weave in ends. Sew buttons opposite buttonholes.

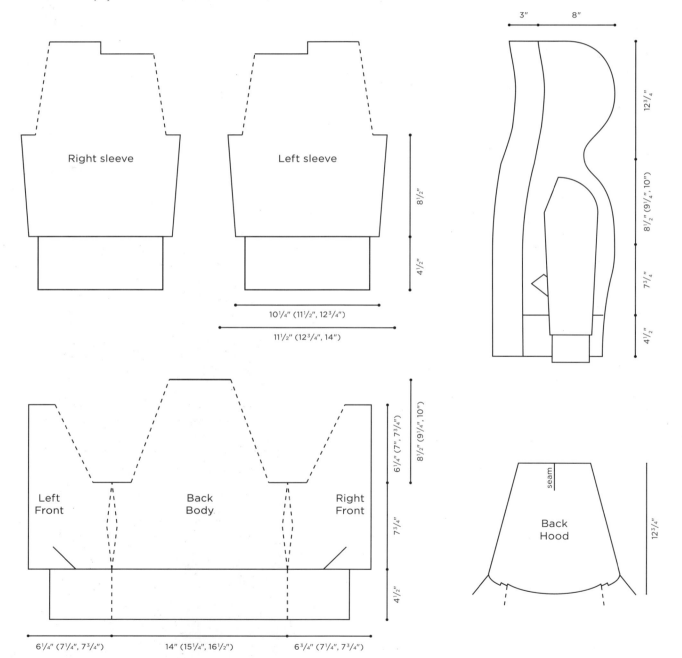

aspen hat

ONE SIZE

KNITTED MEASUREMENTS
Circumference: 20½" (52cm)
Height: 8¾" (22cm)

MATERIALS
1 skein of Twinkle Handknits Soft Chunky
(100% merino wool; 83 yd/77 m per 200 g
skein) in Pink *or* 59 yd/54 m of any super
bulky weight yarn in the color of your
choice

US size 19 (15 mm) 16" (40.5cm) circular
knitting needles

One set of US size 19 (15 mm) double-
pointed needles

Two 1⅜ (3.5cm) buttons

GAUGE
9½ sts and 14½ rows = 6" (15cm) in St st
on size 19 needles.

SPECIAL STITCHES
S2kp: Sl next 2 sts together as to knit, knit
next st, pass 2 slipped sts over; (creates a
straight double decrease).

HATBAND

With circular needles, CO 37 sts. Do not join, but begin working
back and forth in rows.

ROWS 1–2: Knit.

ROW 3: Knit into front and back of first st, knit to end.

ROWS 4–6: Knit.

ROW 7: K2tog, knit to end.

ROWS 8–10: Knit.

CROWN

RND 1: BO 5 sts, pm, knit rem 32 sts. Divide sts evenly onto 3 or 4
double-pointed needles and work in the round.

RNDS 2–3: Knit.

RND 4: K10, s2kp, k13, s2kp, k3—28 sts.

RND 5: Knit.

RND 6: K2, s2kp, k11, s2kp, k9—24 sts.

RND 7: Knit.

RND 8: K7, s2kp, k9, s2kp, k2—20 sts.

RND 9: Knit.

RND 10: K1, s2kp, k7, s2kp, k6—16 sts.

RNDS 11–12: Knit.

Cut yarn. Thread yarn through rem sts and pull tight. Weave in
ends. Allow rounded end of band to overlap and sew buttons
onto band, working through both layers.

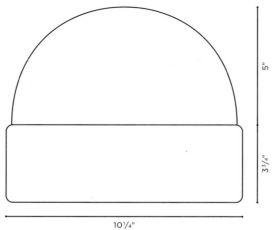

5"

3¾"

10¼"

skating sweater

SIZES XS (S, M, L)

KNITTED MEASUREMENTS
Bust: 22" (24", 26", 28") [56 (61, 66, 71)cm]
Length: 22¼" (23", 24 ", 24¾") [56.5 (58.5, 61, 63)cm]

MATERIALS
5 (5, 5, 6) skeins of Twinkle Handknits Soft Chunky (100% merino wool; 83 yd/77 m per 200 g skein) in Kelly Green *or* 347 yd/ 317 m of any super bulky weight yarn in the color of your choice

US size 17 (12.75mm) and 19 (15mm) 24" (61cm) circular needles

Stitch holders

GAUGE
10 sts and 11 rows = 5" (13cm) in Cabled Rib Stitch on size 19 needles

NOTES
Body is worked in one piece to the underarm. Sleeves are worked in k1, p1 rib. Bring stitches into pattern as increases are made.

SPECIAL STITCHES
R3L (Rib 3 left): S1 next st to cable needle and hold in front, K 2nd st on left-hand needle and leave on needle, P first st on left-hand needle and drop both sts off needle, K1 from cable needle

CABLED RIB PATTERN
RNDS 1 AND 2: *K1, p1; rep from *

RND 3: *R3L, p1; rep from *.

RNDS 4–7: Rep Rnd 1.

Rep Rnds 1–7.

CABLED RIB PATTERN

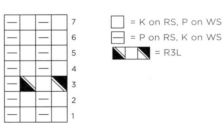

= K on RS, P on WS
= P on RS, K on WS
= R3L

BODY

With larger needles, CO 44 (48, 52, 56) sts. Pm to indicate beg of rnd. Join, being careful not to twist stitches. Begin Cabled Rib Pattern and work even until piece measures 15½" (39cm).

DIVIDE BODY

BO 1 st, work K1, P1 rib in pattern as established across next 20 (22, 24, 26) Back sts, place remaining 23 (25, 27, 29) Underarm and Front sts on holder. Working back and forth in k1, p1 rib on Back sts only, BO 1 st at beg of next 2 rows. Work even 9 (10, 11, 12) more rows.

SHOULDER SHAPING

BO 2 sts at beg of next 4 (4, 6, 6) rows and 1 st at beg of next 0 (2, 0, 2) rows—10 sts. Place remaining back neck sts on a holder.

Place Underarm and Front sts on needle. With RS facing, BO 2 sts, work in k1, p1 rib as established across. Cont in established rib, BO 1 st at beg of next 3 rows—18 (20, 22, 24) sts. Work even 10 rows.

NECK SHAPING

Pattern across 6 (7, 8, 9) sts, join 2nd ball of yarn and BO next 6 sts, pattern across remaining 6 (7, 8, 9) sts. Working both sides at once, BO 1 st at each neck edge twice—4 (5, 6, 7) sts each side.

Work even until Front measures same as Back to top of neck. Bind off.

SLEEVES

(MAKE 2)

With smaller needles, CO 13 (13, 15, 15) sts. Row 1 (RS): K1,
*p1, k1; rep from *. Work 11 (9, 9, 9) more rows in k1, p1 rib as
established. Increase 1 st each side next row. Inc 1 st each side
every 8th row 0 (2, 2, 3) times, every 10th row 2 (1, 1, 0) times
and every 4th row 0 (0, 0, 1) time—19 (21, 23, 25) sts.

Work even until sleeve measures 16" (40.5cm) from beginning.

CAP SHAPING

BO 1 st at beg of next 12 (12, 12, 14) rows—7 (9, 11, 11) sts.
Bind off.

FINISHING

Sew Shoulder seams.

With RS facing and larger needles, pick up 28 sts around
neckline, including sts on holder.

ROWS 1–5: Knit.

ROW 6 (DEC ROW): K2tog, knit to last 2 sts, ssk.

ROW 7: Knit.

ROWS 8–11: Rep Rows 6–7.

Bind off.

Set in Sleeves and sew Sleeve seams. Weave in ends.

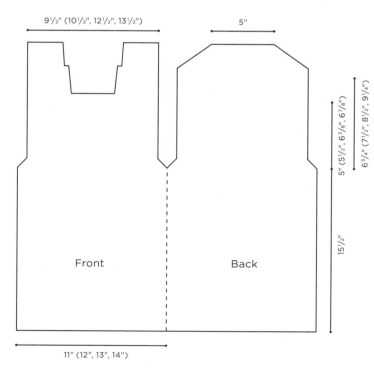

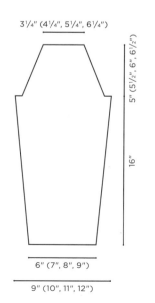

rockefeller sweater

RIGHT FRONT CABLE PATTERN
(OVER 10 STS)
ROWS 1 AND 5 (RS): Ssk, yo, p1, k4, p1, yo, k2tog.

ROW 2 AND ALL WS ROWS: P2, k1, p4, k1, p2.

ROW 3: Ssk, yo, p1, C4L, p1, yo, k2tog.

ROW 6: P2, k1, p4, k1, p2.

Rep Rows 1–6.

LEFT FRONT CABLE PATTERN
(OVER 10 STS)
ROWS 1 AND 5 (RS): Ssk, yo, p1, k4, p1, yo, k2tog.

ROW 2 AND ALL WS ROWS: P2, k1, p4, k2, p2.

ROW 3: Ssk, yo, p1, C4R, p1, yo, k2tog.

ROW 6: P2, k1, p4, k2, p2.

Rep Rows 1–6.

RIGHT POCKET
With larger needles, CO 10 sts. Work Right Front Cable Pattern for 10 rows. Place sts on holder.

LEFT POCKET
With larger needles, CO 10 sts. Work Left Front Cable Pattern for 10 rows.

Place sts on holder.

RIGHT FRONT CABLE PATTERN

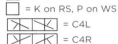
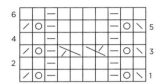

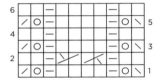

◺ = SSK

◯ = yo

▭ = P on RS, K on WS

▢ = K on RS, P on WS

⬚⬚ = C4L

⬚⬚ = C4R

LEFT FRONT CABLE PATTERN

BODY

With smaller needles, CO 46 (50, 54, 58) sts.

Row 1: K2, *p2, k2; rep from *.

Work 3 more rows in k2, p2 rib as established. Change to larger needles.

Row 5 (RS): P1 (1, 2, 2), work Right Front Cable Pattern over next 10 sts, p0 (1, 1, 2), pm, p10, p2tog, p12 (14, 16, 18), pm, p0 (1, 1, 2), work Left Front Cable Pattern over next 10 sts, p1 (1, 2, 2)—45 (49, 53, 57) sts.

Rows 6–10: Work even in established patterns.

JOIN POCKETS

P1 (1, 2, 2), place next 10 sts on holder and hold in front of work, work in Right Front Cable Pattern across Right Pocket sts from holder, p0 (0, 1, 2), purl Back sts, p0 (0, 1, 2), place next 10 sts on holder and hold in front of work, work in Left Front Cable Pattern across Left Front Pocket sts from holder, p1 (1, 2, 2). Work even 4 rows.

Next row (Dec Row): Cont in established pattern, *work to 3 sts before marker, p2tog, p1, s1 marker, p1, p2tog; rep from * once, work in pattern to end. [Omit (ssk, yo) and (yo, k2tog) portion of cable if necessary]—41 (45, 49, 53) sts. Work even until 28 rows are complete. Sweater measures approximately 11½" (29cm) from beg.

Note: Read through all Neck and Body shaping before continuing.

Next row (Neck Dec Row): P2tog, pattern to last 2 sts, p2tog.

Next row (Inc Row): *Knit to 1 st before marker, m1, k1, s1 marker, k1, m1; rep from *, knit to end—45 (49, 53, 57) sts. Rep Neck Dec Row every 6th row 1 (1, 0) times and every 8th row 2 (2, 3) times.

AT THE SAME TIME when 41 rows are complete, divide for Armholes as follows:

DIVIDE FOR ARMHOLES

Work in pattern across Right Front sts to 1 st before marker, place these sts on a holder, BO next 2 sts, work in pattern across 21 (23, 25, 27) Back sts, place rem 12 (13, 14, 15) sts on holder for Underarm and Left Front.

Working on Back stitches only, BO 1 st at beg of next 2 (4, 4, 4) rows. Work even until Back Armhole measures 4¼" (5", 5¾", 6½") [11 (13, 14.5, 16.5)cm] from beg of Armhole shaping, ending with a WS row.

SHOULDER SHAPING

BO 2 sts at beg of next 4 rows and 1 st at beg of next 2 rows—9 (9, 11, 13) sts. Bind off.

RIGHT FRONT

Place Right Front sts on needle. Beg with WS, bind off 1 st at armhole edge. Cont Neck shaping AT THE SAME TIME, bind

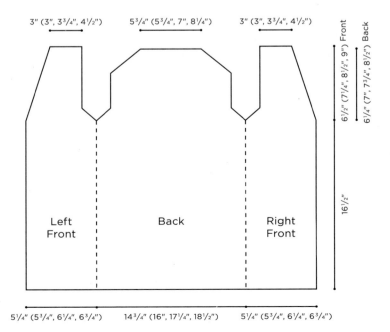

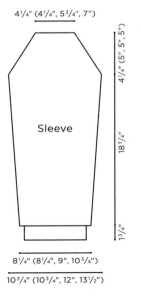

off 1 st at Armhole edge 0 (1, 1, 1) more time—5 (5, 6, 7) sts remain when shaping is complete. Work even until Right Front measures 6½" (7¼", 8½", 9") [16.5 (18.5, 21.5, 23)cm] from beg of Armhole shaping. Bind off.

LEFT FRONT

Place 12 (13, 14, 15) Underarm and Left Front sts on larger needle. With RS facing, join yarn, BO 2 sts, work in pattern to end of row. Cont Neck shaping, BO 1 at Armhole edge on next row. BO 1 st at Armhole edge 0 (1, 1, 1) more time—5 (5, 6, 7) sts. Work even until Left Front Armhole measures same as Right Front Armhole. Bind off.

SLEEVES
(MAKE 2)
With smaller needles, CO 13 (13, 15, 17) sts.

ROW 1 (RS): K1 (1, 3, 1), *p2, k2; rep from *. Work 3 more rows in k2, p2 rib as established. Change to larger needles. Begin reverse St st with a purl row, work even 14 rows.

Next row (Inc Row): P1, m1, purl to last st, m1, p1. Work even 13 rows. Rep Inc Row—17 (17, 19, 21) sts. Work even until Sleeve measures 19¾" (50cm) from beg.

CAP SHAPING

Next Row (Right Side Dec Row): P1, p2tog, purl to last 3 sts, p2tog, p1.

Cont to dec 1 st each end every 3 rows 0, (2, 2, 2) times and every 2 rows 4 (2, 2, 2) times, making WS row decreases as follows: K1, ssk, knit to last 3 sts, k2tog, k1. BO rem 7 (7, 9, 11) sts.

FINISHING

Sew bound-off Front Shoulders to Back Shoulders.

Set in Sleeves and sew Sleeve seams.

POCKET FLAP

Place 10 Pocket sts on needle.

ROW 1: K2, *p2, k2; rep from * to end.

ROW 2: K the knit and p the purl sts. Rep last 2 rows once more. Bind off. Sew sides of Pocket Flap to Body of sweater. Sew Pocket Liners to inside of sweater.

SHAWL COLLAR

With smaller needles and RS facing, join yarn at lower right front edge and pick up and knit 23 sts up Right Front edge, pm, pick up and knit 25 (26, 27, 28) sts from Right Front neck, 10 (10, 12, 14) sts from Back neck, and 25 (26, 27, 28) sts from Left Front neck, pm, pick up and knit 23 sts down Left Front edge—106 (108, 112, 116) sts.

ROW 1 AND 3(WS): P1 (3, 3, 3), *k2, p2; rep from *, p1.

ROW 2: Knit the knit sts and purl the purl sts.

ROW 4 (BUTTONHOLE ROW): K3, p2, k2, p2tog, yo, k2, p2, k2tog, yo, p2, k2, p2tog, yo, work in pattern to end of row.

ROW 5: Work even.

Begin short-row shaping: Pattern to 2 sts before Left Front st marker, wrap and turn, work in pattern to 2 sts before Right Front marker, wrap and turn; pattern to 4 sts before Left Front marker, wrap and turn; pattern to 4 sts before Right Front marker, wrap and turn. Continue short-row shaping in this manner until there are 24 rows at center back. Work to end of row. Final row: BO all 106 (108, 112, 116) sts.

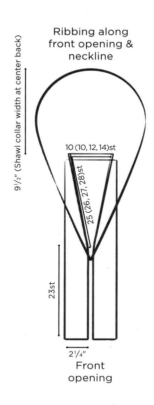

Ribbing along
front opening &
neckline

9½" (Shawl collar width at center back)

10 (10, 12, 14)st

25 (26, 27, 28)st

23st

2¼"
Front
opening

magic shawl

MAGIC CABLE
(OVER 16 STS)
ROW 1 (RS): P2, k12, p2.

ROW 2 AND ALL WS ROWS: K2, p12, k2.

ROW 3: P2, k4, C8L, p2.

ROWS 5, 7, AND 11: Rep Row 1.

ROW 9: P2, C8R, k4, p2.

ROW 12: K2, p12, k2.

Rep Rows 1–12.

= P on RS, K on WS

= K on RS, P on WS

= C8L

= C8R

MAGIC CABLE PATTERN

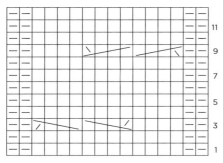

SHAWL
Cable A: With larger needles, CO 16 sts and work Magic Cable for
96 rows.

Bind-off Row: Drop first 2 sts, BO next 12 sts. Fasten off. Drop
last 2 sts.

Allow sts to ladder down to cast-on edge, forming loops. Cut the
center of each loop and tie the two ends together.

Cable B: With larger needles, CO 16 sts and work Magic Cable
for 126 rows. Bind off as for Cable A.

Upper ribbing: With WS facing, pick up and knit 50 sts from one
long edge of Cable A. Row 1 (RS): K2, *p2, k2; rep from *. Work
15 more rows of k2, p2 rib as established. Bind off.

With WS facing, pick up and knit 66 sts from the other long edge
of Cable A. Row 1 (RS): K2, *p2, k2; rep from *. Work 5 more
rows of k2, p2 rib as established.

Keeping fringe on right side, sew sts of k2, p2 rib to long edge of
Cable B, taking care to work into each live stitch of rib. See the
illustration on the next page for an example on grafting the seams.

On right end of shawl, pick up 38 sts.

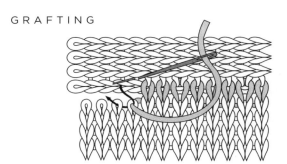

ROW 1 (WS): P2, ★k2, p2; rep from ★.

ROWS 2–11: Work even in k2, p2 rib.

ROW 12 (BUTTONHOLE ROW): Work k2, p2 rib to last 6 sts, yo, k2tog, p2, k2.

ROWS 13–14: Work even.

Bind off.

Repeat for left end of shawl, omitting buttonhole.

FINISHING

Trim fringes to 1 ½" (4cm) each. Stretch rib open and steam to block. Make 2 crocheted chains, each 10" (25cm) long. On WS, sew ends of chains across Cable A as indicated on diagram.

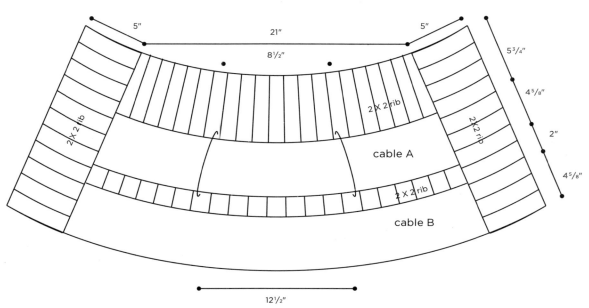

diamond scarf

DIAMOND PATTERN

Row 1 (RS): K1, p1, k1 (ssk, yo) two times, k1, (yo, k2tog) two
times, k1, p1, k1.

ROW 2: K2, p11, k2.

ROW 3: K1, p1, (ssk, yo) two times, k3, (yo, k2tog) two times, p1, k1.

ROW 4: Rep Row 2.

SCARF

CO 15 sts. Work in Diamond Lace Pattern until scarf measures 56"
(142cm). Bind off. Weave in ends.

FRINGE

Cut 32 pieces of yarn, each 24" (61cm) long. Working with two
strands held together attach, 8 sections of fringe along cast-on edge
and 8 sections along bound-off edge.

DIAMOND PATTERN

	= P on RS, K on WS
	= K or RS, P on WS
/	= K2tog
O	= yo
\	= SSK

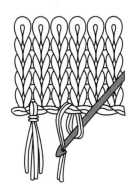

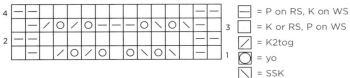

12"   56"   12"

shopping tunic

SIZES S, (M, L)

KNITTED MEASUREMENTS
Bust: 25½" (28", 30½", 33") [65 (71, 77.5, 84)cm]
Length: 25¼" (26", 26¾", 27½") [64 (66, 68, 70)cm]

MATERIALS
1 skein of Twinkle Handknits Soft Chunky (100% merino wool; 83 yd/77 m per 200 g skein) in Black (A); 1 skein in White (B); 1 skeins in Canary (C); 1 skein in Pink (D); 1 skein in Eggplant (E); 1 skein in Coral (F); 1 skein in Baby Pink (G) or 10 skeins of Twinkle Handknits Soft Chunky (100% merino wool; 83 yd/77 m per 200 g skein) in Black *or* 830 yd/770 m of any super bulky weight yarn in the color of your choice

US size 19 (15 mm) 24" (61cm) circular knitting needles

Stitch holders

Stitch marker

GAUGE
9½ sts and 14½ rows = 6" (15cm) in St st on size 19 needles

NOTES
Entire piece is worked in reverse stockinette stitch, then turned inside out to use "wrong" side as right side. Weave in ends on knit side of fabric. The front neckline is formed by short rows.

STRIPE PATTERN

Knit 6 rounds each of A, B, C, D, E, F, and G.

POCKETS

(MAKE 2)
With A, CO 7 sts.

ROW 1 (RS): Purl.

ROW 2: Knit.

ROWS 3 AND 5: With B, Purl.

ROWS 4 AND 6: Knit.

ROW 7: Purl.

Place sts on holder.

BODY

With A, CO 40 (44, 48, 52) sts. Pm to indicate beg of rnd. Join, being careful not to twist sts.

Beg stripe pattern and St st (knit every rnd).

Work even for 7 rnds.

JOIN POCKETS

K1 (2, 2, 3), place next 7 sts on holder and hold in back of work, k7 Pocket sts, k4 (4, 6, 6), place next 7 sts on holder and hold in back of work, k7 Pocket sts, k1 (2, 2, 3), pm, knit to end of rnd.

Work even 5 rnds. Next rnd (Dec Rnd): *K1, ssk, knit to 3 sts before marker, k2tog, k1; rep from * once. Work even 12 (13, 13, 13) rnds. Rep Dec Rnd—36 (40, 44, 48) sts. Work even 7 rnds. Next rnd (Inc Rnd): *K1, m1, knit to 1 st before marker, m1, k1; rep from * once. Work 6 (7, 7, 7) rnds even. Rep Inc Rnd—40 (44, 48, 52) sts

Work even until piece measures 20⅜" (21⅛", 21⅛", 21⅛") [52 (53.5, 53.5, 53.5)cm] from beg, ending last rnd 1 st before marker.

ARMHOLE SHAPING

Bind off 2 sts, k18 (20, 22, 24) Front sts, BO 2 sts, k18 (20, 22, 24) Back sts.

SLEEVE

Pm, CO 14 (14, 16, 18) Sleeve sts, pm, k18 (20, 22, 24), pm, CO 14 (14, 16, 18) Sleeve sts, pm, k18 (20, 22, 24)—64 (68, 76, 84) sts.

Next rnd (Dec Rnd): *K1, ssk, knit to 3 sts before marker, k2tog, k1; rep from * around—56 (60, 68, 76) sts.

Rep Dec Rnd every 3rd (3rd, 4th, 3rd) round 2 (2, 2, 3) more times.

Size M only: Work one rnd even. Next rnd: *K1, ssk, knit to 3 sts before marker, k2tog, k1, S1 marker, knit to next marker, s1 marker; rep from * once.

All sizes: 40 (44, 48, 52 sts). Work even 2 rnds. Place marker at center front.

SHORT-ROW NECK SHAPING

Knit to 3 sts before Center Front marker, wrap and turn (see "Short Rows" on page 78), purl to 3 sts before center front marker, wrap and turn, knit to 6 sts before center front marker, wrap and turn, purl to 6 sts before center front marker, wrap and turn.

Cont in established stripe pattern on all 40 (44, 48, 52) sts until neck measures 13" (33cm). BO loosely.

FINISHING

Turn sweater inside out so that the purl side becomes the "right" side.

POCKET FLAP

Place 7 Pocket sts on needle and work 4 rows k1, p1 rib. Bind off. Sew sides of Pocket Flap to Body of sweater. Sew pocket liners to inside of sweater.

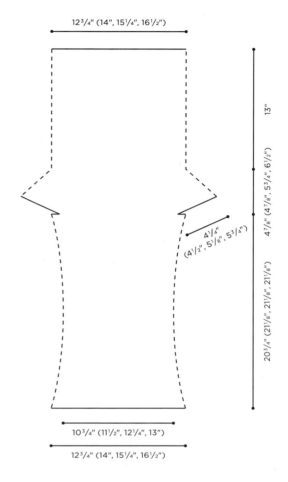

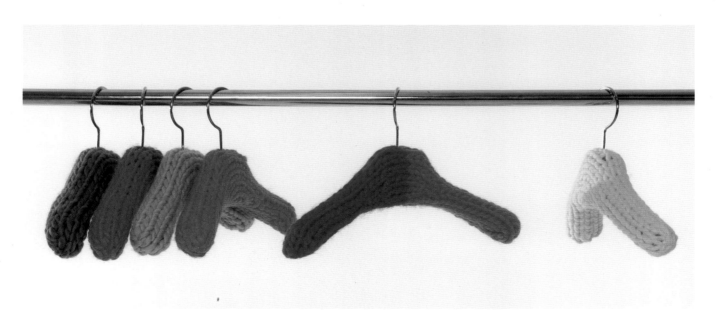

YARN RESOURCES

WHERE TO FIND TWINKLE HANDKNIT YARNS

The yarns I developed for Twinkle inspired me to design the fun and quirky clothing you see in the pages of this book, so I think you'll get the best results if you use the yarns specified. Twinkle Handknit yarns are available at the fine yarn stores listed below, and online at www.twinklebywenlan.com. They are distributed by Classic Elite (check "where to buy" on the www.classiceliteyarns.com website to find a yarn store closest to you). Be sure to call the stores to confirm they have the desired color and yarn before you make the trip. Above all, have fun shopping.

CONNECTICUT
Knitting Central
(203) 454-4300
582 Post Road
E. Westport, CT 06880-4549

GEORGIA
Main Street Yarns & Fibers
(706) 769-5531
16 North Main Street
Watkinsville, GA 30677

Dunwoody Yarn
(770) 394-6404
2482 Jett Ferry Road # 602
Dunwoody, GA 30338

NEW JERSEY
Pure Knits
(856) 401-1232
1501 Old Black Horse Pike T8
Blackwood, NJ 08012-4917

The Knitting Lab
(908) 204-9900
3 Claremont Road
Bernardsville, NJ 07924

NEW YORK
Knitwits
(718) 229-0156
35-16 Bell Boulevard
Bayside, NY 11361

OHIO
Art.Z Knits
(216) 533-2602
27950 Belgrave Road
Pepper Pipce, OH 44124

SOUTH DAKOTA
Yarn Knit
(605) 330-9276
401 East 8th Street, Store # 122
Sioux Falls, SD, 57103

TENNESSEE
Loops
(865) 584-9772
5204 Kingston Pike, Suite 13
Knoxville, TN 37919

Yarniverse
(901) 818-0940
709S Mendenhall Road
Memphis, TN 38117-5212

TEXAS
Hill Country Weavers
(512) 707-7396
1701 South Congress Avenue
Austin, TX 78704

VIRGINIA
Holly Spring Homespun
(804) 598-2232
3837 Old Buckingham Road
Powhatan, VA 23139-7020

WASHINGTON
Great Yarns
(425) 252-8155
4023 Rucker Avenue
Everette, WA 98201

HOW TO CHOOSE SUBSTITUTE YARNS

There are many yarns that can be used as a substitute for Twinkle Handknit yarns. I offer some suggestions below, but if you'd like to try out a yarn that isn't listed, be sure you choose one that is similar in fiber content, weight, and yardage. And, most importantly, be sure your gauge matches the one in the pattern.

For Twinkle Handknit Soft Chunky, Bulky Lopi and Allagash from Reynolds, Baby from Tahki, Magnum from Cascade Yarns, and Burly Spun from Brown Sheep are good alternatives.

Classic Elite Yarn's La Gran and Cascade's Kid Seta are ideal replacements for Twinkle Handknit Kid Mohair.

Instead of knitting with four strands of Twinkle Handknit Cruise yarn, you can use a single strand, such as Jaeger's Pure Cotton; Crystal Palace Yarn's Breeze; Classic Elite Yarn's Bam Boo, Four Seasons, and Provence; and Brown Sheep Company's Cotton Fleece and Cotton Fine.

ABOUT THE AUTHOR

Wenlan Chia is the founder and designer of the fashion label Twinkle by Wenlan. Born in Taiwan, she emigrated to the United States when she was twenty-three.

Twinkle launched in 1999 with in an array of colorful, exuberant chunky-knit sweaters that have become Wenlan's signature. The world of Twinkle has grown to include Twinkle Handknit Yarn, a line of home products named Twinkle Living, Twinkle Accessories, and a fine jewelry collection called Twinkle Jewels.

The collection has been featured in publications including *Elle*, *Harper's Bazaar*, *InStyle*, the *New York Times*, and *Vogue*, among others. Wenlan has received prestigious awards such as the Onward Kashiyama New Design Prize in Tokyo and the Competition of Young Fashion Designers in Paris.

Wenlan currently resides in New York City with her husband, Bernard, and her French bulldog, Milan.